THE MOUNTAINS NEXT DOOR

THE MOUNTAINS

NEXT DOOR

Janice Emily Bowers

THE UNIVERSITY OF ARIZONA PRESS / TUCSON

The University of Arizona Press
www.uapress.arizona.edu

We respectfully acknowledge the University of Arizona is on the land and territories of Indigenous peoples. Today, Arizona is home to twenty-two federally recognized tribes, with Tucson being home to the O'odham and the Yaqui. Committed to diversity and inclusion, the University strives to build sustainable relationships with sovereign Native Nations and Indigenous communities through education offerings, partnerships, and community service.

ISBN-13: 978-0-8165-1243-0 (hardcover)
ISBN-13: 978-0-8165-4699-2 (paperback)
ISBN-13: 978-0-8165-3323-7 (ebook)

Cover design by Leigh McDonald
Cover photo of Rincon Mountains by Denis Fabbrini

Illustrations by Paul Mirocha

Library of Congress Cataloging-in-Publication Data
Bowers, Janice Emily.
The mountains next door / Janice Emily Bowers.
p. cm.
Includes bibliographical references and index.
ISBN 0-8165-1243-4
1. Botany—Arizona—Rincon Mountains. 2. Natural historyArizona—Rincon Mountains. 3. Rincon Mountains (Ariz.) 4. Bowers, Janice Emily. 5. Botanists—United States—Biography.
I. Title.
QK147.B68 1991
508.791 '77—dc20
91-11824
CIP

Printed in the United States of America
♾ This paper meets the requirements of ANSI/NISO Z39.48-1992 (Permanence of Paper).

For Steven again and always
and for Barbara and Pamela at last

Contents

Preface

John Steinbeck said that "the impulse which drives a man to poetry will send another man into the tide pools and force him to try to report what he finds there." A fortunate few reconcile these opposing instincts: they are the writers of natural history, interpreters speaking to the heart with facts gleaned from the natural world. There is a long tradition of nature writing by mystics and philosophers, self-taught naturalists whose biological expertise arises from their sharp eyes and willingness to understand. Here I think of Henry David Thoreau, Joseph Wood Krutch, Annie Dillard and Edward Abbey, among others. Their vision of the natural world, a deeply personal one, is imbued with unspoken ideas: that nature somehow teaches us how to live, or that it contains a hidden message for those who probe deeply enough, or that it is a foil for our personalities.

Countering this is a second tradition, often practiced by scientists like Howard Ensign Evans and Rachel Carson, that largely eschews a philosophical or mystical framework. Such writers try instead to present unvarnished nature in all its complexity and interrelatedness. Their agenda, not at all hidden, is education and conservation, and they are well aware that without the first, the second must fail.

Some of the essays that follow are intended as a dialogue between these two schools of nature writing. Others tell the story of a two-year project I undertook in the Rincon Mountains near Tucson, Arizona: how I came to work there, what I saw, what I learned. The book's three sections—The Flora, The Mountain, and The World Beyond—roughly reflect this progression. The end notes contain references, technical information and opposing viewpoints that did not fit smoothly into the text. In their entirety, these essays examine what it means to be a natural scientist, and they ask the unanswerable question, What is the meaning of nature?

I am indebted to Steven McLaughlin for carrying always the heavier load, both on the trail and off; to Roy Johnson, who started it all; to John McLaughlin for packing plant presses up Mica Mountain; to Hal Coss and Mary Robinson for logistical support; to Margaret Kurzius-Spencer for honesty and for asking questions; to Pamela Portwood and Barbara Kingsolver for sharing manuscripts and lives; to Bill Stewart for finding *Chimaphila maculata*; to Heather Urry for going against her natural bent; and to Tim Priehs and the Board of Directors of Southwest Parks and Monuments Association for financial support. Barbara Kingsolver, Steven McLaughlin, Gary Nabhan and Pamela Portwood helped give this manuscript its present shape, and I am grateful to each of them for their gentle criticisms and thoughtful comments.

THE MOUNTAINS NEXT DOOR

Coming Home

The longest way round is the shortest way home.

PROVERB

I

Halfway between Seattle and Tacoma lies Dumas Bay, a tiny bite out of the Puget Sound shoreline where red-winged blackbirds warble invisibly amid the cattails, and sandpipers scurry up and down the muddy beach. Looking west across the sound, past the smudge pot buoys where seagulls perch and preen, past an enormous boulder shaggy with mussels, past the occasional barge and its tugboat symbionts, you see, if it's a clear day, the Olympic Mountains floating on the horizon, a long line of blue peaks roughly torn from thick paper.

Like the Delectable Mountains of *Pilgrim's Progress*, they beckon, they promise, and when you finally arrive, they will not disappoint. Summer-fat marmots waddle onto rocktop perches, sparrows trill from streamside willows, and deer pause in their browsing and lift their heads into the air. Meadows knee-deep or even shoulder-high with wildflowers make you yearn, like Dorothy in the Land of Oz, to stretch out prone and fall into poppy dreams. Streams tumble down scree slopes into circular basins where drifts of glacier lilies chase the retreating snow. Walking through cloud banks, you squeeze clouds in your hands, collect their droplets on your tongue. Moisture is everywhere, squelching underfoot and dripping overhead. That eerie, mocking, elusive spirit of high, empty places is everywhere, too, and as you toil from an alpine cirque to a knife-edge saddle a thousand feet above, the massive peaks loom and press from every side, no longer safe and pretty like a postcard picture, but immediate and threatening in more ways than you can comprehend at that moment.

These were for a time the most delectable mountains I had ever seen, made more so by unfamiliarity and yearning: because I lived in a faraway desert, they remained a sight to visit, never a place I could think of as home. Their remoteness let me romanticize them as I could not romanticize the mountains I saw from my own front yard. This was not bad in itself; yet, acclaiming the unfamiliar, I inadvertently lost touch with my deepest sources of nourishment. I forgot that the familiar may yet have unfamiliar aspects, that the better I know something, the more deeply I can explore it.

All this I learned once again in the Rincon Mountains near Tucson, a place I had belittled as a homely contrast to the real mountains up north. Because the Rincons have never felt the sculpturing hand of glaciers, they have no looming, snowy peaks, no bowl-shaped tarns, no knife-edge ridges. Dryness is their signal characteristic. Clouds skim high overhead, untouchable, unknowable. Most days, rainfall is a mere rumor, a phenomenon read of in books. Sparse rainfall means scarcity of surface water. Except for the few permanent springs, what little water exists is apt to disappear underground during the dry seasons.

Because they lack superficial beauty, the Rincon Mountains are not well known. You don't see postcards of them in local drugstores alongside the ubiquitous photographs of barrel cacti, rattlesnakes and jackalopes, nor do tourists flock to them from far-flung points of the globe. Even people who have lived next-door to them for years know nothing more of these mountains than their name. On a map or from the air, the Rincon Mountains are shaped like an L, but from the city, the three major ridges line up on the horizon like goods in a bakery display case, two lumpy loaves of French bread and a brioche, prosaic as toast, unromantic as an electric oven.

This is a neighborhood mountain range, more a place for family picnics and teenage beer busts than mountaineering expeditions, a fact made painfully obvious when you hike to the top and look back down on the Tucson basin. You may be surrounded by wilderness—most of the range *is* an official wilderness area—but it is hard to feel wild when, six thousand feet below, you see the grid of city streets through the smog and can imagine all the rest—the sirens and rumble of traffic, the crowded parking lots and impatient motorists. Five hundred thousand people live in that valley, and every year their housing developments and shopping centers and industrial parks creep closer to the mountains, which serve as a scenic backdrop and a namesake for subdivisions.

Neither remote nor wild, then, the Rincon Mountains have become a backyard convenience. Packs of feral dogs roam Saguaro National Monument, and, on weekends, cadres of survivalists dressed in camouflage hold training exercises involving semiautomatic weapons. Vandals destroy equipment at the visitor center weather station, and riders from a nearby dude ranch have eroded certain trails into knee-deep ruts. Only the absence of roads saves the range from even worse despoliation. One superintendent did plan a road from the bottom to the top: it was to be his legacy. Fortunately, this project never materialized, and the only way to see the higher elevations is still on foot via the hundred miles of trails.

No scenery to speak of, a chronic shortage of water, threatened by suburban sprawl, difficult of access: it seems the Rincon Mountains have little to recommend them. When I gave them enough time and effort, however, they became delectable in their own way. Often, back in Tucson after three or four days in the high country, I would stare at them as I drove or walked through town. Pale blue in the mornings, obscured by city haze, indigo in the afternoons, every boulder outcrop sharply focused by the slanting sun, they seemed impersonal and uninhabited. You would never guess that five thousand feet above you a massive rock dome sheltered small, magenta primroses, that violet-green swallows swooped at dusk over a glassy pond, that watchful deer sank hoof-deep into a sedge-filled meadow. Having only recently dipped my toes into dark pools and clambered up stairstep canyons, I possessed this intimate knowledge, and, as it must, knowledge eventually brought love.

2

I came to work there by a circuitous route that began in childhood. Although my parents were not outdoor people and did not hike, hunt, fish or camp, they liked to tour the California countryside, and on rare spring Saturdays they would take my sister and me on wildflower drives. Equipped with coffee cans half-filled with water to keep the flowers fresh, we would head east toward Lytle Creek or north to Antelope Valley or back of Redlands into the foothills of the San Bernardino Mountains. I especially loved these rolling, grassy hills, green in the winter after rains had wet the soil, and tawny in the summer when one hot and cloudless day followed another and the very air seemed tinder-dry, on the point of bursting into flame.

As we drove in the flickering light between tall rows of blue eucalyptus trees, I would spot the most beautiful flower in the world, and I would shout, "Stop, Daddy, stop." I would run back to it through tumbleweeds that scratched my legs and dust that coated the toes of my shoes, usually to find a handful of chicken feathers caught on barbed wire or a wad of Kleenex disintegrating on a stick. But once in a while it would be an evening primrose, broad and white like a china bowl, or a cluster of spectacle-pod with flowers as sweet as bath powder.

Sometimes we traveled over the hills and beyond, out to where the desert tilted upward from either side of the highway like a drafting table, and here we would find fields of owl's clover, acre after acre of magenta flowers as though a giant bucket of paint had been overturned. Or we would see pastures lush with lupines and poppies and tidy tips and fiddle-neck and dozens of others whose names I didn't know but craved as a cat craves a bird.

My parents fed my wildflower hunger as best they could. Mother bought me field guides and showed me how to press my collections between pages of newspaper weighted down by dictionaries and encyclopedias. Father took my coffee-can bouquets to a botanist he knew and scribbled down the names as fast as she rattled them off. Even so, some hungers are never satisfied, and mine for names of plants aches inside me yet. All the flowers I saw in books as a child but never found—snow plant with its neon red corollas glowing like a brand; golden trident with its umbels of yellow stars; kinnikinnik with its name like the clicking of castanets—some part of me, unappeasable, yearns for them still.

After childhood, I put wildflowers behind me as I, like many of my generation, embarked on a compassless search for direction. I was too young to have become a beatnik, too cautious to become a hippie. By the time I turned twenty-one, my life seemed to be little more than a series of false starts. Then one day some breath of orange blossoms on the wind, some dream of poppies like a river of fire called me back to where I started and made me remember wildflowers. I searched used bookstores until I found a copy of Willis Jepson's *Manual of the Flowering Plants of California*. Even in those days, it was out of date, but that hardly mattered. My goal was to learn the names of wildflowers, not to become a botanist. Finding that the formal, technical language of the manual made little sense, I bought another book, *How to Identify Plants*, and memorized it from cover to cover.

Like any autodidact, I suffered from the gaps in my education, and I made all the typical beginner's errors, taking meadowrue for maidenhair and hopelessly confusing the various species of rabbitbrush, burroweed, snakeweed and turpentine brush, all those yellow-flowered look-alikes that go by the despairing appellation of DYC's—Damn Yellow Composites. My first taxonomy class at the university was, therefore, a relief and a revelation, like learning to read. I fell into it the way I fall into every new enthusiasm: headlong, pell-mell, to the neglect of all else. From the first day of classes, I loved the dissecting microscopes that magnified the tiniest stamen to the size of a pea. I loved the mothball smell of the herbarium, where dried and labeled plant specimens were stored in tall metal cabinets. I loved the exquisitely precise words used to describe plants: scabrous, verrucose, villous, canescent, cordate, secund, paniculate. I loved the sonorous Latin names of plants and discovered I could remember them as easily as the names of my friends.

After I graduated with a degree in botany, I scratched out a little niche for myself. Have plant press, will travel, was my motto as I collected and identified plants, compiled floras, mapped vegetation, matched old landscape photographs, published technical papers.

Perhaps foolishly, I assumed I would be a botanist always. When you're snug at home, you don't expect disaster. The botanical projects eventually petered out, though, and I couldn't afford to wait for another one. I found work in an office and tried to be grateful that I was employed. I folded my blue jeans and put them at the bottom of a drawer, retired my hiking boots to the back of the closet. But like an ant that hitchhikes on your boot and becomes so far removed from its origins that the universe no longer contains a place for it, I, too, felt I had no legitimate place on earth. To confess, "I'm not a botanist anymore," was as much as saying, "I no longer exist."

Perhaps I never would have found my place if it had not been for Roy Johnson, a research scientist with the National Park Service and a friend whose faith in me was deeper than my own. He suggested that I apply for a small grant to do research in the national parks. With no great expectations, I wrote a proposal for a project in Saguaro National Monument, a sixty-three-thousand-acre preserve in the Rincon Mountains just east of Tucson, Arizona. My research was to be a flora of the monument, a catalogue of all the plants that grew within its boundaries. I could keep my office job while working in the mountains on weekends.

After I submitted the proposal, I tried to forget about it. Sometimes, though, driving through the city, I'd glimpse the Rincon Mountains and remember. Then I'd glance away, unwilling to recognize their silent challenge. Unhappy as I was at the office, it was at least a familiar misery, while in the mountains awaited unknown dangers as well as those too easily imagined: wildfires, rattlesnakes, rabid skunks, black bears, feral dogs. And every time I looked at my own body, heavy and lethargic after months of inactivity, I knew that the biggest obstacle was myself. How could I carry a forty-pound pack from the bottom of the mountain to the top when I could hardly walk across campus without losing my breath? I wondered as well if I'd retained my botanical skills. Was identifying plants like swimming, something you would always know how to do? Or was it more like learning a language, knowledge that fades when you never use it? At times I hoped my proposal would be approved, but most of the time I prayed it would not, and when Roy telephoned one day to say that the project had been approved, I was torn between anxiety and joy.

I was coming home again.

3

I worked in the Rincon Mountains for two years and made thirty-eight excursions into the range—some for two or three days at a time, many more for a single day—and no trip was like any other. Each stands out in memory for some unique feature—something beautiful or frightening or crazy or funny. There was the trip when I sprained my ankle, another when I assiduously avoided seeing a bear that was equally determined not to see me, a third when, by breaking and entering government property, I showed an unsuspected aptitude for crime. Other trips remain forever identified in my mind with particular plants. Just as avid baseball fans can tell you the game situation of crucial innings fifteen years after the fact, and bridge players can recite hand by hand the brilliant play that won them a tournament weeks or months before, botanists remember the locations of all their outstanding collections, and I doubt I will ever forget the Rusby primrose trip, the crested coralroot trip, the Rocky Mountain maple trip.

The first trip—a day hike up the Tanque Verde Ridge trail—stands out because it *was* the first, and because it was a homecoming.

It was one of those gorgeous April days that almost reconcile you to the interminable desert summers—sunny but not hot, and just enough breeze to ruffle your hair. The trail started in the midst of desert vegetation—small, brushy trees called paloverde for their green bark, and treelike cacti, the saguaros that give the monument its name. Despite the trees, the plant cover was so sparse that the terrain took on the drab hues of rocks and earth. Above the desert, scattered oaks and junipers stippled the tawny slopes with olive. Where oaks and pinyons crowded together, the stippling merged to a uniform bottle green. Higher still, the forest of ponderosa pines and Douglas firs painted an indigo swath over the topmost peaks and ridges.

Winter rains had been scant that season, so I didn't expect centerspread displays of wildflowers, nor did I find any. In draws, around boulders and under trees, though, wherever a little extra moisture had gathered, enough bloomed to make it seem like spring. Many were old favorites, wildflowers I had known and loved since childhood: California poppy with glossy orange petals as silky as an areola; brittlebush, with yellow flowers lifted in a hemisphere above the globe of gray leaves; desert lupine with petals an indefinable shade between blue and purple, the color of a summer sky an hour after the sun has set. Bulbous, black carpenter bees, as ponderous as garbage trucks, fumbled among the flowers, and honeybees buzzed self-importantly from plant to plant.

Absurdly nervous at first, I kept dropping things—my field notebook, my sunglasses, my pen, my plastic bags. Names of plants I once knew as well as my own had unaccountably slipped my mind. After the first twenty minutes of uphill walking, my legs hurt and I couldn't catch my breath. What had I gotten myself into? I sat panting on a boulder while my husband, Steve, a seasoned botanist, poked among the rocks and returned with handfuls of plants.

"Here's wild mulberry," he said, "do you have that on your list yet? What about the phlox? Did you get that? Do you want me to save this phacelia? The fruits are immature, but maybe you can identify it anyway."

His enthusiasm finally kindled mine, and, forgetting my tiredness, I hopped from boulder to boulder after him, our old rivalry and partnership established once again.

"Look, I found cream cups," I called.

"Where?"

"Right there."

"There? How could I have missed it?"

By the end of the day I had made twenty-eight collections and filled up the first ten pages in my field notebook. These pages record each collection by name and number, list additional plants not collected, mention the vandals and feral dogs, and even record the weather for that day. Properly scientific and objective, they say nothing about the large uncertainties and small triumphs of a homecoming. Yet reading them now, I remember how the collecting bag bumped companionably against my leg, and I can feel once again the slickness of poppy stems, the stiff serrations of bear-grass leaves. I hear Steve's voice calling out plant names faster than I can record them, and I hear my own voice calling back the names of more old friends.

I remember, too, how the uncertainties melted away. What remained was the unalloyed joy of being a botanist again.

Collections

A fingering slave
One that would peep and botanize
Upon his mother's grave.

WILLIAM WORDSWORTH

I

Now that I am nominally grown up, I no longer collect by stuffing coffee cans with wildflowers. I stuff plastic bags, instead. All sizes come in handy—sandwich bags for the smallest plants, gallon bags for almost everything else, and trash-size bags as containers for the rest. Nor do I still press plants by piling *Webster's* and *Bartlett's Familiar Quotations* on yesterday's newspaper. My plant press is now an alternating stack of blotters and corrugated cardboards, all cut to a standard twelve by eighteen inches. Between each blotter and cardboard I lay half a sheet of newspaper, folded down the middle, and inside each sheet I place a single specimen, trimmed as necessary to fit the space. I try to find a middle ground between the slapdash botanists who cram so much plant material in each sheet that roots and leaves dangle from the press, and those compulsive souls who treat each specimen as a work of art, carefully arranging the flowers and snipping off branches that spoil the effect. I number the newspaper sheets to correspond with numbers in my field notebook; each specimen has its own number and that will be its number always. When I'm done, I tightly strap the stack of cardboards, newspapers and blotters between two wooden covers.

I've become so accustomed to this process that I forget how peculiar it looks to others. I was pressing plants on the tailgate of my pickup truck once when a man came crashing through the wild roses below my campsite. As he held up his stringer of trout, perhaps to offer me some, he noticed my press disemboweled across the tailgate and blurted, "What the hell are you doing?" Another time, hiking with friends, I spied a luscious evening primrose, eggshell white and tissue fragile, blooming in damp sand. Automatically, I bent down to collect it, when one of my companions cried, "Oh, can't you leave it alone for once?" I complied, startled that my curiosity and delight struck others as thoughtlessness and greed.

I refrained from pointing out that John James Audubon, it's said, would sometimes shoot a hundred birds for the sake of a single painting, and that John Xántus, during his twenty-one-month stay at Fort Tejon, California, collected 1,794 bird skins, 145 mammals, 229 containers of fishes and reptiles, 211 nests, 740 eggs, 107 bottles of insects, and 14 bales of pressed plants. This isn't the carnage it may appear. Xántus's specimens—and those of most legitimate collectors—ended up in the plant, bird and mammal collections of universities and museums where they're available for study. Students use these collections to check tentative identifications. Taxonomists rely on collections when preparing monographs, which requires examination of thousands of specimens to see how they vary from place to place and individual to individual. Conservationists use collections to help them assess the status of rare organisms and decide how best to protect them. Scientific illustrators often make their precise and detailed drawings from collected specimens. In the end, the scientific value of plant and animal collections outweighs the unnatural deaths of so many living creatures.

Yet even born collectors may sometimes view their natural impulse with dismay and something akin to loathing. Henry David Thoreau wrote that he once kept three pieces of limestone on his desk, but when he discovered that they required daily dusting, he threw them out the window. He had, he implied, transcended the ignoble urge to squirrel away treasures. In this (as in other) ways, Thoreau proved disingenuous, for at his death his friends discovered that his attic room housed drawers full of arrowheads, rocks, nests, eggs, dried flowers and other effluvia from Concord's tideline.

The urge to collect is human, atavistic, impossible to over-come. I can hardly remember a trip to the mountains when I didn't carry away pine cones heavy with seed and resin, nor a trip to the beach when I failed to return with pockets or paper bags full of seashells and polished rocks and gnarled roots. Nowadays, I dump my shells into a wide, shallow basket and seldom look at them again. As a child, though, I had a real seashell collection, a small cabinet of tiny drawers divided into three compartments, each just big enough to hold a single shell, and although I never open the little drawers to look at the razor clam, which I found before its olive green sheath had worn away, or to gaze at an aba-lone the size of a thumbnail yet perfect in every detail, I cannot bear to let them go.

We collect in order to possess. Seashells, pine cones, min-erals, butterflies, rhododendrons, books, kitchen gadgets, china figurines, incunabula, paperweights: they fill our shelves and drawers, cover our walls and tabletops. We can never have enough of them; in fact, the more we have, the more we need. They anchor us, somehow—connect us to the past or fill the empty spaces in our lives.

We collect in order to prolong the present, as though by saving this particular leopard-spotted cowry we could hang on forever to that day at the beach when wind and salt spray stiffened our hair and shorebirds dashed up and down with the swash like mechanical objects on a magnetic track.

We collect in order to partake of something larger than our-selves. Standing on a slip of a trail, snowy peaks looming around us, wide-mouthed valley opening below, a solitary raven glid-ing overhead as its shadow undulates over the snow, we want to shout, to weep, to pull it all closer to us, to exchange substances or even be swallowed entire, as a snake devours its prey. With Edna St. Vincent Millay we might cry, "O world I cannot hold thee close enough." Being merely human, we settle for a rock, a pine cone, a feather, a flower, knowing that this part will have to stand for the whole.

2

Nowadays collecting is the purview of students, of compilers of floras and of good botanists everywhere who remain curious about the plants around them. But nineteenth-century collectors seldom compiled floras; scoring new species was their goal. They scoured the West, then largely unexplored, by foot, horse and train, vying with one another in the number of new species and sheer bulk of specimens amassed. There were no plastic bags in those days, of course; collectors stuffed plants into vasculums, lidded tin cylinders that could be slung over the shoulder by a strap. They didn't have aluminum and nylon backpacks either; their pack frames were wood, the pack itself a heavy, bulky canvas bag.

As professional collectors, most earned a living by selling their specimens to museums and universities, a practice that has largely died out. They made multiple sheets of every collection, often as many as thirty or forty from one location. The more specimens they collected, the more they could sell, and there are tales of early collectors simultaneously discovering and extirpating new species.

The bounty of undiscovered plants sometimes attracted the packrat types, men like Edward Palmer, who not only amassed some one hundred thousand plant specimens, but somehow found time to save coins, newspaper clippings, Indian pottery and chips knocked off historic buildings. Most collectors were less scattered, although a few, like Adolph Wislizenus, were undeniably scatterbrained. As a civilian, he traveled west with troops during the Mexican-American War, slipped across the border into Chihuahua and was promptly taken prisoner. His indulgent captors let him collect in the local area, and when he crossed back over the border, he brought a number of new species with him.

Despite their undeniable tendency to collect for collecting's sake, men like Palmer, Wislizenus and many others are not quite analogous to Granny poking through yard sales for yet another china teapot. Almost by default, these early collectors became explorers in unknown territory, confronting grizzly bears, hostile Indians and a thousand other dangers. John Frémont watched helplessly as a flash flood swept away half of his fourteen hundred specimens and severely damaged the remainder. David Douglas fell into a pit and was gored to death by a bull. There were easier ways to earn a living. No sensible person collected solely for the money involved. Glory was part of their motivation: what better remembrance than to have your name immortalized in a Latin binomial? John Gill Lemmon, a Civil War veteran who rediscovered his childhood love of wildflowers after war injuries left him an invalid, alternately sent his collections to one professional botanist, then another, according to whoever named the most "lemmonis." Deep inside, however, even Lemmon did not collect for glory alone. A helpless victim of his passion, he was drawn as irresistibly to wild plants as salmon to their spawning grounds—a perverse kind of homing instinct that made him abandon the comforts of settled life for months at a time.

Most nineteenth-century collectors were by and large not men of science, so, like Lemmon, they generally sent their specimens to professional botanists for identification, specialists who built their careers and reputations on the willing backs of the field men. Cacti often went to George Engelmann, a German-born doctor who practiced in St. Louis. In photographs, his plump cheeks, light-bulb nose and tonsure of a beard make him look every inch the prosperous German burgher he was born to be, but somehow he developed instead a dual expertise in obstetrics and cacti, naming new species in between deliveries, I suppose. Other plant families were frequently sent to Asa Gray, the great taxonomist who from his throne at Harvard ruled North American botany for decades. Still others went to Edward Greene, Gray's western rival. The two men could agree neither on taxonomic philosophy nor on the new, burning question of Darwinism. Their rivalry, it seems, extended even to their appearance: the clean-shaven Greene, beaming and bespectacled above his clerical collar, could hardly have presented a greater contrast to the rugged, bearded, hawkeyed Gray, handsome enough (but far too dignified) to be a movie star.

COLLECTIONS 17

I could wish for more female models among the early botanists of the West. Sara Plummer Lemmon was one of the first,
but little is known about her. With her husband, John, she collected in southeastern Arizona when the beleaguered Apaches
were at their fiercest. The Lemmons botanized with perfect im-
punity, however, since the Indians took the couple's inexplicable
interest in plants as a sign of insanity. John named a delicate
rock fern after Sara, little enough recompense for the woman
who shared all the rigors of fieldwork yet endured the indig-
nity of having their specimens distributed under the rubric "J. G.
Lemmon and Wife."

More is known about fierce Kate Brandegee, largely because
she made so great an impression on her mostly male colleagues
that memoirs of her abound. Old photographs contradict their
descriptions of her as an emasculating virago. Her soft eyes and
serious mouth suggest instead a woman in love with botany—
and one determined to make her way as a scientist in what was
very much a man's world. That she did, despite others' continual
efforts to undercut her. She earned a medical degree and started
the California Botanical Club; named many plants and had many
more named after her; edited the botanical journal *Zoe*; and became curator of botany at the prestigious California Academy
of Sciences, where she took charge of the herbarium, a kind of
library of pressed plants. She left a legacy any botanist, male or
female, would be proud of.

Kate's assistant at the California Academy of Sciences was
Alice Eastwood, deceptively photographed in old age as a sweet
little librarian, white-haired and demure, hardly a heroic figure;
yet as a young woman she single-handedly rescued, sheet by
sheet, the contents of the herbarium during the 1906 San Francisco earthquake and fire.

The flora of the West is largely known now, so descriptions
of new species have slowed to a trickle. The automobile has replaced the horse as the conveyance of choice, and Apaches require
permits to collect on the reservation. No one thinks twice about
a woman's editing a scientific journal. We no longer combine

obstetrics and taxonomy, nor do we sell our collections. Still, these are my people, this is where I belong, and I recognize in my own passion for wild plants the faint reverberation of their resounding song.

Roses by Other Names

But these young scholars who invade our hills . . .
Love not the flower they pluck, and know it not,
And all their botany is Latin names.

RALPH WALDO EMERSON

I

When I described the herbarium to a friend—the windowless basement room, the dried specimens mounted on stiff paper and filed in large manila folders, the rows of gunmetal gray cabinets so closely placed that two people can hardly pass between them, the dissecting microscopes like praying mantises about to pounce—she said, "Ugh—that doesn't sound very appealing."

She was right, but somehow the contrast between living plants and pressed specimens has never bothered me. Their colors may have faded, their leaves may be brittle, their sap may have dried up, but seen through a dissecting microscope, pressed plants reveal complex and unexpected beauty. Under magnification, an abrasive leaf is seen to be covered with stiff, curved, translucent hairs like Velcro. A stem with stickers turns out to be armed with stilettos, each darkened at the tip as though by a drop of dried blood. The random streaks on a petal become a zigzag design in bargello needlepoint. The faint indentations on a seed are craters on the moon.

Looking at plants through a dissecting microscope, subtly aware of the mothball smell of the herbarium, the sheets of brittle brown specimens, the old labels handwritten in sepia ink, I lose track of time. I no longer hear the fluorescent light buzzing overhead or the phone ringing in the curator's office. I'm aware only of the intricate puzzle set before me and of the impossibility of pitting equivocal words against intractable plants.

To find the name of an unknown plant, a botanist uses a key, a printed series of choices that come in pairs. At each pair, she decides which choice best describes the specimen at hand. Successive decisions eventually lead her to a plant name, a tentative identification, which she then checks against the specimens in the herbarium. Simple as it sounds, the process is far from automatic. Frequently she's forced to make subjective decisions, such as leaves that are "very hairy" or only "somewhat hairy." Sometimes the alternatives are not clear-cut: if the choice is between flowers ten to twenty millimeters long or flowers fifteen to twenty-five millimeters, the specimen at hand inevitably has eighteen-millimeter-long blossoms. Occasionally it's impossible to apply the choices to the specimen at hand: orange versus yellow sap, for example, isn't revealed by a dried specimen. Often flower color cannot be determined either, because many pigments, particularly the blues and reds, are fugacious and fade rapidly after pressing. (The careful botanist, of course, prevents this problem by routinely noting flower color in her field notebook.) Sometimes the terminology mystifies: euphorbias don't have petals but petaloid appendages; their flowers are clustered into cyathia and the cyathia are borne in pleiochasms. It is easy to pick out the beginning taxonomy students in the herbarium because they spend as much time looking up enigmatic terms in the glossary as they do peering through the microscope.

Once in a while I spend literally hours on a single specimen for one reason or another: it's missing crucial parts, perhaps, or the key is inadequate, or I am not seeing what I need to see. As I work I combine calm ratiocination with feverish intuition, and when I finally come up with the indubitably proper name, it's with a feeling of triumph, like the *Arabian Nights* storyteller who dives deeper and deeper into her interlocking tales, then spirals upward and emerges at last with the triumphant conclusion.

When I began collecting seriously, I thought I wouldn't bother with the Latin names of plants—too hard to pronounce, too difficult to remember. But I quickly learned that a single species may have a dozen common names or, more often, none at all, and that a single common name often applies indiscriminately to five or six unrelated plants. Scientific nomenclature sweeps this confusion aside by providing each species with one and only one valid Latin name. That is why the red-flowered morning glory I collected in the Rincon Mountains still goes by the same name that Linnaeus, the great Swedish botanist, gave it 250 years ago. He meant only one thing by the words *Ipomoea coccinea*—this particular wild vine with oboe-shaped flowers and trefoil leaves. That's the power of a scientific name—it fosters unambiguous communication about organisms, a conversation that spans generations without losing clarity or precision.

I am obsessed with names, at times. Like any good field botanist, I can name thousands of different plants on sight: some to genus only (which is akin to recognizing that the radio is playing something by Bach), many more to species (which is like identifying the *Third Brandenburg* Concerto). On steep, exhausting trails in the Rincon Mountains, when it was all I could do to put one foot in front of the other, I would recite the name of each plant as I passed it—*Blepharoneuron tricholepis, Pinus cembroides, Arctostaphylos pungens, Garrya wrightii*. The names became my mantra, a marching song in dactyls and trochees. Knowing a multitude of names is sometimes reassuring. Almost anywhere I go in the Southwest, I see one old friend after another out my car window, and I feel grounded. I know where I am because I recognize the plants around me. At other times it is merely boring—nothing left to identify, nothing new to learn. Time to move to a place where all the plants are mysteries. That is the danger of knowing names—assuming that because you have learned the Latin name of an organism you know everything about it. Then you become like the birders who dash back and forth across the state, the continent and the world, pausing just long enough to add another bird to their life-list. They forget (or never knew) that naming is not the same as understanding. Names are the basis of biology but not its substance.

2

Three hundred years ago, modern-day science was in its infancy, and so little was understood about most plants and animals that to know their names *was* to know nearly everything about them. Naming organisms was a major scientific preoccupation. Given that plant species alone number some two hundred and fifty thousand, this is not a task I would want to assume. Yet this is the job that Linnaeus took upon himself. He botanized throughout his native Sweden and across northern Europe, and he sent his students around the world to bring back as many plant and animal specimens, living and dead, as their ships' holds could carry. Based on this bounty, he put names to eleven thousand organisms.

Linnaeus was much more than the Swedish Adam, however. He invented our present system of binomial nomenclature, in which a plant or animal is given both a genus and a species name, assigned to the delphiniums, for example, and more specifically categorized as *Delphinium nelsoni*, Nelson's delphinium, or *Delphinium cardinale*, the red delphinium. Over and above this, Linnaeus devised a scheme for assigning plants to genera and species. Artificial as this system was (it made no attempt to group plants according to their relatedness, which is why we no longer use it), his was the first comprehensive and practical arrangement for classifying and identifying organisms. This was his greatest accomplishment: to organize a cosmos out of chaos.

In those days, the main drawback to the Linnaean system was not its artificiality, but its depravity, for Linnaeus announced to the world the sexuality of plants. He did more than announce it, in fact: he rolled in it, gloried in it, positively exulted in it. As an adolescent (the timing is no doubt significant), he had been vividly struck by the fact that every flower contains genital organs. This fascination continued into adulthood, when he devised his sexual classification system. It wasn't enough, however, for him to divide all flowering plants into twenty-three classes; he had to give each a perverse little twist. The class Monandria—plants having one stamen per flower—represented "one husband in a marriage." The Diandria could be thought of as two husbands in the same marriage and so forth, up to the Polyandria, where there were "twenty males or more in the same bed with the female." As if this weren't bad enough, he discoursed at length about the flower-head of pot marigold, which he placed in the class Confederate Males with Necessary Polygamy, where "the beds of the married occupied the disk and those of the concubines the circumference, the married females are barren and the concubines fertile."

Naturalists who relied on Linnaeus's system found themselves accused of licentiousness and worse. According to the Reverend Samuel Goodenough, a British cleric, "nothing could equal the gross prurience of Linnaeus's method." He said it shocked female modesty. Naturally, no proper lady would have allowed herself to be tainted by the gross prurience of Linnaean botany, but dedicated nature lovers like Dorothy Wordsworth, sister of the poet, let the controversy swirl about them unheeded. Her diary tells us that on one of her walks she noted a "pretty little waxy-looking Dial-like yellow flower," which she identified several days later according to the Linnaean system as *Lysimachia nemorum*, the yellow pimpernell. The Reverend Goodenough notwithstanding, her female modesty resisted with equanimity the assault upon it. You can't keep a good botanist down.

3

The desire to know the names of the plants and animals around us must be among the most natural of human impulses. Long before Linnaeus devised his binomial system of nomenclature, people around the world had already named and classified all the important plants and animals in their environment. The noun—the name—is, after all, basic to human thought, and therefore to most other activities. How can you bake bread if you have no words for flour and yeast? How can you weave cloth if your vocabulary doesn't include loom, warp, weft, shuttle, and thread? How can you forage for food if your vocabulary won't let you distinguish between the edible mushroom and the poisonous toadstool?

So Adam began to name. But he didn't name everything. Most folk taxonomies take into account about five hundred plant genera, fewer plant species. This is partly a matter of practicality: in preliterate societies, knowledge is passed on verbally, so the catalogue of names must be small enough to be memorized. It's a matter of common sense, too. The plants that stand out—those good for food, fiber, fuel, medicine and magic, and even some harmful ones, the weeds and poisonous plants—receive names. The rest remain a green blur—unprofitable, therefore unremarked and unnamed.

Folk classifications, designed to communicate information, categorize organisms according to their uses. For this reason, folk taxonomists tend to be extreme splitters with the most useful plants and extreme lumpers with everything else. The Sahaptin Indians of the Pacific Northwest, for example, named just 10 percent of the plant species in their area, but when it came to vital plants like the Indian root, a staple food, they were extremely precise and put names to fourteen different species where botanical taxonomy recognizes only twelve.

Linnaeus essentially codified folk taxonomy, giving it a Latinate polish. At the time, he had no idea of the almost infinite diversity of the living world. (No one did.) He had in mind a system that would account for, say, five hundred or eight hundred genera, a catalogue you could carry around in your head. Having no conception that the number of plant and animal species on this planet, give or take a few thousand, is ten million, he brought forth a toothbrush to scrub down an elephant. Now, after nearly three centuries of steady classifying, scientists have named no more than 15 percent of all the species extant. Even more staggering, taxonomists are so few and the current pace of environmental degradation is so rapid, it seems likely that 80 percent of the planet's species will be extinct before we have added another 5 percent to our inventory. The elephant's right foot is squeaky clean, but what about the rest of it?

In theory, the scientific name of an organism is our passport to a wider world of ideas and information. Armed with the Latin binomial, we should be able to acquire limitless knowledge about a particular plant or animal. Its taxonomy, ecology, morphology, evolution—all should become open books. In practice, however, 99 percent of named organisms are appallingly obscure. We know their Latin binomials and little else.

It is popular to blame the taxonomists for this state of affairs. Naturalist Joseph Wood Krutch, seeking to learn more about the spadefoot toads that materialized in his backyard after summer rains, found almost nothing in the scientific literature other than their name. Taxonomists, he concluded, had concentrated on describing new species to the exclusion of all else because "the distinguishing of species is a relatively easy as well as a gratifyingly esoteric business." Drawing on the popular stereotype, he implied that taxonomists are gray, precise little men who seldom leave the confines of their trig and sterile laboratories. I can sympathize with his frustration: I have gone countless times to taxonomic monographs hoping for even minor insights into pollination or evolution and been disappointed.

But taxonomists, feverishly working with the system they inherited—Linnaeus's toothbrush—have little time for these alluring byways.

Some scientists have heretically suggested that maybe it doesn't matter if we never complete our catalogue of the living world. What *is* in a Latin binomial, after all? Not much, when you consider the living, breathing, eating, excreting, reproducing organism itself. What *does* matter, these scientists say, is not names but information: how does the organism interact with other organisms? how does it function as a discrete cog in the environmental wheel? how big a gap will its extinction create? They urge a new kind of taxonomy in which information, not identification, is the primary goal.

Quit naming, start learning. It's good advice. But *can* we quit? That's the point. We are classifying animals. The need to name is built into our brains, so much so that neurologists have a term—visual agnosia—to describe people who cannot recognize familiar objects and faces—who cannot name nouns. How pallid and frustrating their lives must be, like that of the patient who, handed a rose, knew it only as "a convoluted red form with a green linear attachment."

The plan to name and catalogue each of ten million species is a futile one: like a roomful of monkeys randomly typing out the collected works of William Shakespeare, it would take more years than life has existed on earth. It smacks of outrageous hubris, too, a profoundly egotistical act. In naming a plant or animal, we essentially state, "We decide who or what you are." On the other hand, since we find nothing remarkable in bestowing individual names on each of the four billion people on this planet, giving names to each living species seems not so ambitious in comparison. Seen in this light, naming plants and animals is profoundly self-effacing. The act recognizes that other creatures exist, that they have names and therefore a legitimate claim on our attention. Every name we apply is yet another badly needed recognition that we, *Homo sapiens*, are one among ten million.

Backwards into Spring

Spring—an experience in immortality.

HENRY DAVID THOREAU

The first snowfall of the season brings wintry colors to the Rincon Mountains. In its double blanket of leaf litter and snow, the woodland is, for a day or two, brown and white like an old, old quilt. Turpentine brush, a mass of golden blossoms in the fall, turns to tawny fluff, and the grasses, so green and vivid after summer rains, subside to rust and brown. A few last, purple fruits ornament the prickly pears, but most are long since gone, devoured by coyotes, rodents and javelinas. White twigs of cottonwood gleam in the sun, and the yellow leaves also seem burnished. As small shadows race across the ground, you look up expecting to see butterflies, then realize that these are the shadows of falling leaves.

On top of the mountain, where several feet of snow accumulate after big storms, winter is a time of quiescence. Plants and animals rest and endure, possessing their souls in frigid patience until the spring. But at the bottom, snow is rare, and winter is a time of preparation, a brief period of transition from the endings of autumn to the beginnings of spring.

If we are lucky, winter brings rain to the desert. Chilly, soft and gray, winter rains soak ever deeper into the soil until every crevice and cranny is saturated. These are quiet storms with none of the bluster and braggadocio of summer thundershowers. The bowl of the sky becomes one vast, gray stratocumulus, an endless sieve endlessly dripping. Woolly clouds gather over the Rincon

Mountains and brood for days on end, finally parting to reveal white slopes that last for an hour or a day or a week.

Winter tourists grumble that they could have stayed in Portland if they wanted rain. The fact that we have 350 sunny days a year is no consolation to those whose vacation coincides with the 15 wet ones. Luckier visitors find our climate to be all that was promised and fill their days with golf and horseback riding. Even so, they are surprised that our winter nights are undeniably cold and that frost rimes roadside weeds and windshields early in the morning. They are even more surprised that the mulberries and sycamores along Tucson streets have yet to shed their leaves in the middle of December. Could this be winter? And if so, what happened to the fall? They would be more amazed still if they traveled out into the desert and saw that many native plants—the green-barked paloverdes, the twiggy wolfberries, the drought-enduring creosote bush—respond to winter rains by sprouting new leaves. Like the tourists, they cannot afford to waste a single warm, sunny day. Underground, the rains are having an effect, too, as wildflower seeds imbibe moisture, swell and crack.

The turn from January to February begins the transition from winter into spring in the Rincon Mountains. It starts softly, inconspicuously, like the preliminary rustling in the strings at the beginning of the *New World* Symphony. Indian plantain, a grassy looking annual, spreads a green mist across the ground, filling in the empty space between creosote bushes. Next, the four-petaled yellow flowers of bladderpod appear and the lavender ones of filaree, tiny flowers that, massed in thousands, transform plain homespun into calico.

As February turns to March, spring crescendos. The mustard family takes possession of slopes and flats alike—twistflower, lacepod, peppergrass, London rocket, wild mustard, none spectacularly beautiful in themselves but all welcome as harbingers of the season. The borages, too, tiny white or yellow flowers on fiddle-neck stems, grow rank under trees and shrubs. Their acidulous hairs break off into the fingers of anyone incautious enough to collect them without gloves.

By April, all the stops are out. It's a family reunion out there as mustards and borages are joined by composites, umbellifers, hydrophylls and many others. You would need a gaudy palette to paint them properly: there's nothing subtle about the strident magenta of owl's clover, the vivid purple of stinking phacelia, the blatant orange of California poppy, particularly when they mix together in a glorious, tasteless melange, as vulgar as a sunset and just as exhilarating.

Before the season ends, perennials add their color to the annuals. Wild onion, its paper-white petals delicately striped with pink, thrives among the needle-tipped rosettes of shindagger, where the wild pigs known as javelina cannot scrounge out the small, pungent bulbs. Flowers of indigobush, massed in thousands, stain hillsides the color of crushed raspberries. The yellow or white cups of mariposa lily balance on long, fragile stems like crystal goblets.

As April turns to May, desert wildflowers dry up and blow away. But the symphony is not over yet. Now, as paloverde blooms, a yellow wave billows across the desert and laps against the base of the mountains. Mesquite blooms, too, and you never knew there were as many bees in the world as you see working the creamy spikes of a single mesquite tree. Late spring is also the season for cactus blossoms. That cacti flower now, at the hottest, driest time of year, seems like a metaphor for something, and maybe it is. A simpler explanation is that desert annuals must germinate, flower and set seed before the soil dries out, but cacti are not so constrained. They can bloom late in the spring because their stored water makes them more or less independent of soil moisture. Paloverdes and mesquites are able to flower late, too, because their deep roots tap moisture stored well below the surface. By blooming at the end of the season, these plants face less competition for pollinators, and the warm temperatures of June help mature their seeds.

By the time the last saguaro blossom opens and closes, spring in the desert is over. But you can keep pursuing it, if you wish, as it seeps upslope like liquid up litmus paper. Hiking from the bottom to the top of the Rincon Mountains, you can track certain species through all stages of bloom, from ripening fruits in the desert to wide-open flowers in the woodland to developing buds in the forest. It seems you are climbing backwards and forwards at the same time: forwards into the day and backwards into spring.

To be aware of wildflowers is to be keenly aware of time's passing. Every January photographer friends in Illinois call to ask whether the desert will bloom this spring. Not being God, I have no absolute knowledge, but based on how wet and warm it's been, I can make a good guess. Most years, I warn them to keep their expectations low, since most years are, by definition, average. Only an extraordinary year evokes the kind of displays they are hoping for; they want calendar shots of endless fields of wildflowers so dense they hide the ground. Such a year comes every four decades, it's said, which calls up a vision of the stock of scenic photographs dwindling to dangerously low levels.

Desperate for photo opportunities, my friends plan their itinerary so they can follow the spring as it travels from the low desert along the Colorado River to the higher desert around Tucson, but most years their careful arrangements are to no avail. In August you can drive from place to place in search of wildflower displays, a strategy that works because summer rains are so spotty that one neighborhood may be afloat under two inches of rain while another, five miles distant, is perfectly dry. But winter rains generally cover a broader area. When they come, they come for the just and unjust alike. When they fail, they fail for everyone, and botanists and photographers have no choice but to wait for a better year, however long that may take.

Old-timers insist that the spring of 1941 was the best they have ever seen. I don't go back that far, but even so, I cannot imagine how that spring could have outdone the back-to-back extravaganzas of 1978 and 1979. To meet with one fabulous spring after ten years of desert living was wonderful; to experience two in a row was a revelation. The combination, literally rarer than a blue moon, resulted in a bumper crop of wildflowers the second year, partly because so many seeds had been set the year before.

In that glorious spring of 1979, I visited the sandy deserts of northwestern Baja California, an arid land where there is hardly enough rain most years to cover the bottom of a kettle; but I found myself knee-deep in wildflowers. When I sat down in the midst of them, I disappeared from sight. Magenta rivers of lupine flowed down dry washes, and on sandy flats the large white petals of evening primrose were packed as closely as cells in a honeycomb. That was the best spring ever, even though the sheer abundance of bloom made the desert seem emptier than ever after the flowers were gone.

These extraordinary seasons are predicated upon complicated combinations of temperature and rainfall because each wildflower species has particular requirements for germination. Rains that come in late September or early October, while temperatures are still warm, bring forth lupines, evening primroses and wild phloxes. Chilly December rains favor the mustard and borage families. Fiddle-neck wants nights close to freezing and a quarter inch of rain. Woolly daisy prefers slightly warmer nights, mild but not warm days, and at least half an inch of rain, unless some rain has already fallen that winter, in which case a quarter inch will do. When the rains do come it is often when temperatures are too warm or too cold, in which case the wildflower displays are usually disappointing.

Even when a variety of seeds do germinate, the rains often forsake the desert too soon and the seedlings wilt, then die without setting seed. (If this happened year after year, the seed bank would soon be depleted.) The climatic lottery leaves wildflowers no choice but to hedge their bets. They do this with chemicals that impregnate the seed coat. Seeds of most desert annuals won't germinate until all of the inhibitor has been leached away, which requires a substantial rainfall of at least a quarter inch in some cases, a full inch in others. The seeds are capable of lying dormant for decades, if necessary, waiting for the single downpour that will ensure soil moist enough to carry them through their entire life cycle.

Seeds are as alive as you or I while they wait in the soil; they are in a different state, that's all, a ten-year syncope or coma. As they wait, they respire, the slowest of all possible metabo-

lisms in a snail-paced race to see whether they will consume all
the endosperm that keeps them alive before the first germinating
rains come.

Like Rip Van Winkle or Peter Pan, they fool time. They dis-
perse not only through space, scattering themselves around the
parent plant, but through the seasons as well. They are tiny time
travelers from earlier springs, waiting the chance to deliver their
message—not Time is Money, but Time is Life.

Time is a hidden variable in every biological equation. Blazing-
star flowers open so precisely at four o'clock in the afternoon that
bees hover outside, waiting for the petals to roll back; cicadas
live as nymphs underground then emerge as adults after seven-
teen years; human fetuses require nine months of gestation inside
their mothers' wombs: all depend as much on time as if it were
visible or tangible, the one-hundred-and-fourth element on the
periodic table.

That any plant or animal species even exists is partly a function
of that mysterious element, time. A series of fossil ammonoids,
snail-like denizens of ancient seas, show time and the environment at work. Examining one ammonoid after another, you can
see how the decorative embellishments on their shells become
more and more elaborate over the millennia. You can see how
some species eventually abandoned the traditional shell shape and
uncoiled into tusks or ramshorns. You can see all this because
the gradual evolution of hundreds of ammonoid species has been
preserved in compressed and hardened sediments, layered rocks
that we interpret as a time-line stretching across five hundred
million years.

A compiler of floras, not a collector of fossils, I seldom consider such vast expanses of time. When I collected in the Rincon
Mountains, time haunted me by its very paucity. Assembling
a flora became a rush against nature's calendar as the seasons
changed so fast I could hardly keep up with them.

Time for me was linear, a succession of days, weeks and
months to be organized as efficiently as possible. It was something I could run out of. But the natural world never runs out
of time. For plants and animals, time moves in a cyclic fashion,

from sunup to sunup or spring to spring. Sometimes I wished that, like the desert wildflowers, I could fool time. But having no mechanism for dormancy, I could hope only for enough seasons to carry out the work I loved. Only then, once I had finished— all my collections identified and labeled, all my notes compiled into a final list, the list itself safely consigned to the pages of a botanical journal—could I rest. I would then have sown a time capsule of my own, something that would last far longer than I.

Pulling Summer
from the Ground

Even the most hardened liar won't defend this
summer climate.

WILLIAM A. CANNON

I

Summer begins unpropitiously here. Every year we all agree we cannot remember such a hot summer as this one. Even early in May, temperatures of 100°F are nothing uncommon. Each day brings us nearer the solstice, when our hemisphere will be as close to the sun as possible. An unwilling Icarus, I would turn around if I could. The heat builds into early July, when daily temperatures reach 110°F or more. I threaten to move to Alaska. During this entire period, no rain falls. Not a drop. We forget what rain is like. I threaten to move to Seattle.

The paloverdes first shed their pinhead leaflets, then, as the dry season continues, jettison a few twigs, and, if relief still fails to come, sacrifice branches or entire limbs. Perched along knobby stems like small bow ties, the paired leaflets of creosote bush take on bronze tones. Wolfberry, ocotillo, brittlebush and whitethorn become collections of bare twigs. Even the prickly pears droop, and their pads wrinkle and yellow. The prolonged buzz of cicadas, as imperious as a jackhammer, issues from treetops, a sound as harsh and dry as the air itself.

Fieldwork in this season, the arid foresummer it's sometimes called, is a penance rather than a pleasure. Even early in the day, walking uphill is hard, hot labor, and you quickly soak your clothes through with sweat. Little stays the conscientious botanist from her appointed rounds, though, so one May morning, my twelve-year-old daughter, Heather, and I dutifully set out along the Manning Camp trail in the Rincon Mountains. The day started badly and deteriorated from that point. Heather, having misplaced her tennis shoes, wore an old pair of mine, but they were too tight, and her toes banged painfully into the tips with every step. As always in May, swarms of gnats blanketed our arms and legs no matter how often we brushed them away. May is snake season, too, and when a tiger rattlesnake buzzed us, a trill of fear galvanized my skin. "Zero at the bone," as Emily Dickinson put it.

Heather dislikes hiking even at the best of times, and by mid-afternoon our conversation consisted largely of complaints on her part and curt rejoinders on mine. "Look at it this way," I finally said. "These are probably the worst conditions you'll ever find for hiking. It's hot, there are all these bugs, we're sweaty, our feet hurt, there are rattlesnakes—the only thing that could make it worse would be to run out of water." Not too much later we did, May also being the season of large irritations and small disasters.

About the time you think you cannot bear it any longer, the summer switches into phase two. Cauliflower clouds tumble across the sky, colliding silently overhead but dropping no rain. You feel like Tantalus in Hades, unable to drink the water or eat the fruits so teasingly close at hand. Some years the rains fail to materialize altogether. The late, hot spring grades imperceptibly into the early, hot autumn with no wet, hot summer in between. Until our summer rains start, we languish in a season when, no matter what the calendar says, the days are too warm for spring and the rains are too scanty for summer, a season that tests our love for the desert.

The first few storms are usually dust storms. Lightning plays mumblety-peg with the ground, and thunder growls some distance away, but it's all crash and flash, as dry as a cracker-eater's whistle. As the air pressure drops and the wind picks up, the front door, the kitchen door and the back door slam one after another. Gusts roil up the dirt, and gardeners watch helplessly while their top soil departs for the next county. Palm fronds, cardboard boxes, plastic bags and styrofoam hamburger cartons hurtle through the air like disorderly flocks of geese, and flying birds, as they head for cover, tumble about like rubbish. You step outside for a moment, clenching your eyes against the dust and grit, to check the likelihood of rain. It's raining somewhere, you can smell it: the odor of rain-dampened earth arrives faintly on the wind like music from a distant radio station. You can see it, too, off in the distance, a fringe of rain trailing underneath gray clouds, blessing someone else's neighborhood. Half an hour later, the storm—what there was of it—has dissipated, leaving nothing but the neighbor's trash.

The violence of the real storms, when they finally do hit, never ceases to astonish and even frighten me. At first, fat, slow rain-drops plop like large, juicy bugs on your windshield, bounce off the street like water on a hot griddle. After a few minutes the tempo picks up, and soon rain is pounding hard and fast on pavement and rooftop, sluicing along the curbs, filling gutters that haven't run for five months or more. The air becomes thick with rain, so thick you can't see more than a few yards in front of your car. There's nothing to do but pull over, since the wind-shield wiper that can clear visibility through sheets of driving rain has yet to be invented. An inch of water washes over the highway, and big trucks spray plumes that envelop your car as they whoosh by.

It's better to be at home. After you've dashed from room to room cranking the windows shut, you can relax and watch the drops batter the glass. The swamp cooler, a rooftop box that pushes water-cooled air into your house, barely works in this humid weather, so you turn it off and and open the door. Cool air rushes in through the screen. Through the open door you watch silver threads of lightning in the black sky. Thunder rumbles closer and closer. Water rises in the street, filling it curb to curb within the hour. Sirens, the inevitable accompaniment to rain in Tucson, wail from several directions. You are grateful to be in here, not out there shooting the rapids at Alvernon and Grant. As the storm zeros in on your house, you can count no space of time between the blinding flash and the deafening crack. Lights flicker, the stereo wavers. Time to gather candles, matches, flashlights. By the time you have located them all, the worst has passed. If it's the first storm of the season, you want to interact with it. You rush outdoors in your swimsuit, stand in the yard like a child as rain slicks your arms and legs, drips off your hair and lashes, splashes your legs. Rain pelts so hard you can hardly catch your breath, as if you had waded chest-deep into an icy lake. If you're caught on the trail, you have no choice but to interact, keeping in mind that bare skin dries faster than blue jeans and that, in an electric storm, standing in an open field is as dangerous as seeking shelter under the tallest tree. In camp you can always retreat to your tent and fret about the puddle in one corner, since designers of tents seem no more able than manufacturers of windshield wipers to deal with southwestern downpours.

After urban cloudbursts, grackles and English sparrows and house finches regroup. Their chatter fills the trees, a gladsome noise. The air is cool and moist and fragrant with the scent of creosote. The cat appears from an unknown hiding place, disgruntled but perfectly dry. Checking your backyard rain gauge, you are astonished at how little water it's collected—most of the rain blew right over the opening. The next morning, winged ants swarm at eye level and green fig beetles bumble into cars and windows and screen doors. Out in the desert, chocolate brown millipedes glide over the rocks, their eyelash legs in continuous motion like the tread of an earth-moving machine. Furry red mites speckle the dirt, animated confetti. Mated dragonflies zip overhead, pretzels with a purpose.

Life has returned to the desert.

It's the rains that send summer trickling down the stream beds, that pull it out of the earth. All the trees and shrubs that had lost their leaves sprout a new crop. After the summer rains begin, seeds that lay dormant since they were shed last fall, that slept soundly through winter's rains and spring's renewal, soak up water from the soil and swell and soften until they crack. Their tiny white roots ferret deeper into the ground, and yellow cotyledons work between grains of dirt and shove to the surface.

Summer rains also invigorate the perennial grasses that look like lifeless clumps of straw most of the year. Like most blessings, this one is mixed. Grass fountains overhang Rincon Mountain trails, and grass pollen, invisible but pervasive, hangs in the air. Red dots stipple my legs where grasses swish against them—an epidermal reaction that reminds me of the scratch tests that allergists administer—and my nose begins to drip and my eyes to itch. On the other hand, as open slopes turn unwontedly green, I am free to imagine for a month or two that I know what it's like to live in Pennsylvania. As I hike, I chant the names of summer grasses, a kind of found poem: dropseed, sprangletop, three-awn, wolftail, bluestem, tanglefoot. I admire their architecture, designs so intricate that only the finest of nibs could draw them: the toothbrush precision of hairy grama spikelets, the windmill spikes of feather grass, the deliciously furry heads of rabbit's foot grass, the formidable awns of tanglefoot and three-awn, strong enough to pierce the lining of a cow's mouth—strong enough, too, to curl into tight corkscrews that plant themselves in response to changing humidity.

Once summer rains start, the oak woodland, usually an old sobersides, comes into its own. Drunk with rainfall and warmth, it goes wild, a televangelist on a toot. Cerulean morning glories spring out of the ground and clamber up mesquite trees or drape themselves over stumps and fences. Wild beans take a page from *Jack and the Beanstalk*, growing faster than watermelons on a Texas truck farm. The yellow-headed composites indiscriminately called sunflowers by the layman (but known to the botanist by a dozen different names) choke clearings, pastures and roadside ditches. Scarlet creepers, a morning glory with a tubular red flower, coil up sunflower stems and twine around the heads, flowers upon flowers, as good an emblem as any for the season and the place.

2

After the rains finally come, bringing summer with them, I remember why I tolerate the heat and the gnats and the rattlesnakes. For the burst of summer wildflowers, that's why. During the arid foresummer months of May and June, my collections in the Rincon Mountains drop precipitously. I come home with only a dozen different species to show for a long day's hot and sweaty effort. But once summer rains start, I can hardly bring enough bags to hold all I find. On one trip I made fifty-four collections, most new to my list, on another, seventy-six. The irritations and disasters of fieldwork fade in comparison to the wonderful richness of the summer flora. I respond like a seagull to fish heads—with instinctive rapacity and ferocious delight—and I fix my mind upon the reasons why a small, unremarkable mountain range should support upwards of nine hundred plant species.

The existence of two major flowering periods is one. In southeastern Arizona, most annuals are either spring bloomers or summer bloomers because their germination depends on temperature. Spring-flowering annuals germinate when the soil is moist and cool, summer-flowering species when it is moist and warm. Few species can germinate at both times: you don't find poppies in the summer or morning glories in the spring. By dividing the environment seasonally, hundreds of species of wildflowers can coexist in the same small area between February and November.

Another reason is variety in rock types. Most of the range is schist or gneiss, granitic rocks compressed and deformed deep within the earth. At several places, however, limestone rocks, bent and folded like ribbon candy, have been thrust to the surface. In Posta Quemada Canyon the limestone is furrowed as though by fingers dragged through wet clay, pitted like paw prints in mud. The landscape itself, its ridges and ravines, its spurs and saddles, is repeated in miniature on the face of every rock. Limestone is rough in other ways, too: its chemical constituents are too harsh for many plants, and water is more difficult to extract than on granitic rocks. Oddly, many plants that do grow on limestone often cannot be found on other substrates. The first time I botanized in Posta Quemada Canyon, half my collections were new to my list, all denizens of limestone found nowhere else in the range.

There is yet a third reason for the richness of the Rincon Mountains flora. Sixteen different species of the grass genus *Muhlenbergia* grow there, some quite difficult to tell apart without the aid of a dissecting microscope and a good key. The significant difference between mountain muhly and New Mexico muhly, for example, is whether the tiny floral bracts have three teeth apiece or only one. This could hardly be a matter of earth-shaking importance for their survival in the wild, you would think, and you might reasonably wonder why we need both mountain muhly and New Mexico muhly in the Rincon Mountains, much less the other fourteen. We don't. But evolution in its ceaseless convolutions and complications has given us not only these sixteen, but, on a worldwide basis, some one hundred more, as well. Species evolve in isolation yet seldom remain alone for long. As they migrate, they mix, and in mixing they form biologically diverse communities. Much as a ripening pear is a sink for sugars manufactured by the leaves, the Rincon Mountains have been a sink for plants, not just species of *Muhlenbergia*, of course, but of oaks and grama grasses and lip ferns and many more.

But perhaps the primary reason for the large number of species in this small mountain range is the simple fact that the top is 5,500 vertical feet above the bottom. A Swedish ecologist named Olof Arrhenius once suggested that species richness is a function of area: the larger a place, the bigger its flora. According to this model, Organ Pipe Cactus National Monument, which embraces five hundred square miles of southwestern Arizona, should have twice as many species as the Rincon Mountains, which cover half as much area. Yet the opposite is true: the Rincon Mountains flora is twice the size of the Organ Pipe flora. Arrhenius's model does not work in the Southwest. Here, topographic relief, the difference in elevation between the bottom of a mountain and its top, counts for more than area, and since the Rincon Mountains possess substantially more topographic relief, their flora is much richer. As relief increases, the number of habitats increase, too—slopes of different aspect, canyons, rock walls, talus, creek beds. Plants respond in kind. Deer muhly is a grass of seasonally wet stream beds, while the aptly named cliff muhly prefers rock walls. Arizona muhly thrives on open, gravelly slopes. Bamboo muhly seems to prefer the shade of trees and cliffs. When relief is great enough, the climate becomes diversified, too. Temperatures drop and rainfall rises the higher you climb, creating distinct climatic zones on sizable mountain ranges. Again, species select various sections of the climatic gradient according to their needs. Porter's muhly is a desert grass. Mountain muhly requires a wetter, cooler regime, and thrives best in mountain meadows. Diversity of habitat and climate mean increased living space for plants, and the result is more species in a given place.

The result of all this for me is more work, of course, but I don't mind. My idea of hell is a chemically clean monoculture—mathematically straight rows of cotton or sorghum flipping past the car like fenceposts, no weeds, birds or insects, no irregularity of any kind, nothing for my eye to hold and caress. When my flora is enriched, I am enriched, for it is only human to love diversity, multiplicity, fullness, variety.

3

The need for variety seems to be engineered into our genetic blueprint; babies develop best when stimulated with a variety of colors, shapes, sounds and sensations. Still, there is a danger in overstimulation, for both babies and adults. Joseph Wood Krutch said that as an aid to awareness, new sights and wonders, like other stimulants, must be used with caution. "If the familiar has a way of becoming invisible, the novel has a way of seeming unreal—more like a dream or a picture than an actuality. . . . Madder music and stronger wine pay diminishing returns."

Thoreau knew this, and he was content with the mild music and unfortified wines that Concord afforded. It's not difficult to flip open his journal at random and find him engrossed in something so ordinary most of us would pass it by without a glance.

"As I went under the telegraph wire, I heard it vibrating like a harp high overhead," he writes on September 3, 1851, and again five months later, "When the zephyr, or west wind, sweeps this wire, I rise to the height of my being." Such revelations were the beneficent result of having no money, he believed. Unable to travel widely, he had been "made to study and love this spot of earth more and more." Three years later, when a well-meaning acquaintance suggested that he travel abroad, he could not be persuaded. "I fear the dissipation that travelling, going into society, even the best, the enjoyment of intellectual luxuries, imply," he responded. "If Paris is much in your mind, if it is more and more to you, Concord is less and less, and yet it would be a wretched bargain to accept the proudest Paris in exchange for my native village." Do you want to go wide or do you want to go deep? Those seem to be the choices. Thoreau chose to go deep. Staying in one place, he learned minute particulars about the lives of the bullfrog, the fox, the blackbird, the bee. The familiar was rich for him because he mined it for everything it had to offer. Also, he knew that while his surroundings remained the same, he himself changed, and this gave him a new outlook on common sights.

Compiling a flora is a quintessentially Thoreauvian activity, involving continual reexploration of the familiar. Walking the same trails time after time, year after year, I often found plants I had missed before, proving to myself what Thoreau already knew: that the familiar, explored deeply enough, continues to bring new insights. That's what he meant by saying he'd traveled much in Concord. Much of my pleasure in the Rincon Mountains came from hiking the old familiar trails that never changed and were always different. Sweating on the Manning Camp trail in August, I would recall the blustery, chilly days of early winter. Crossing the dry creek bed in June, I would remember the tumbling freshets of the summer before. Walking up the Miller Creek trail month after month, I loved to stop by all my special nameless places. This is the pool where I saw the garter snake, I would think, that's the stretch where I startled a lizard into the water. Earlier this spring, phacelia spread in a sky-blue pool under those mesquite trees; now it's thick with autumn sunflowers. The bedrock cistern where Heather caught a frog one month had shrunk considerably the next, and streamers of algae as fine as hair drifted across the water, while two moths, like flowers with half their petals missing, floated on the surface. I watched the seasons march through the canyons, followed the wildflower parade from February through November, and throughout it all realized that I could travel in the Rincon Mountains forever and never learn all they contained.

The Island Life

*In the life of each of us, I said to myself, there is a
place remote and islanded, and given to endless
regret or secret happiness.*

SARAH ORNE JEWETT

Mica Mountain, the highest point in the Rincons, hardly quali-
fies as a peak at all. The view from this broad, gently sloping
dome is mainly of trees—a forest of young, vigorous ponderosa
pines as thick as tent caterpillars in their sturdy cocoon. The pines
sprouted more or less simultaneously after a severe forest fire a
few decades ago and have since grown just tall enough to block
your view. Standing on tiptoe, which is your automatic reaction,
does not help. Only if you had a jet pack on your back and could
rise fifteen or twenty feet above the trees (or if you were willing
to climb the rickety fire tower bolted to Mica Mountain bedrock)
could you see beyond and below them.

Better for views—and for the dizzying, tip-tilting, edge-of-
the-world sensation you expect on mountaintops—is Rincon
Peak, the second highest point in the range. It really is a peak,
a huge cone of a mountain that might, from its shape, be the
remnant of a volcano. The broad base flares like a skirt; sandy
washes tack it in place, stitching it securely to the fabric of the
desert. Rising rapidly, the slopes gather into the tiny peak itself, a
nipple of bedrock and broken boulders 5,200 feet above the desert
floor. Cliffs spiral around the rocky cap like iron steps around a
lighthouse. If not for a fortuitous break in this balustrade, climbing Rincon Peak would be an escapade strictly limited to rock
climbers. As it is, the trail takes you directly to the top, though

not without effort, which is just as well; a good view is one you should be required to earn.

And earn it you do. Parts of the trail lie on slopes so steep that you ascend on hands and knees, especially in the summer, when, after weeks of daily rains, the soil is pure mud, slicker than a bar of wet soap, kept in place only by the roots of Douglas fir and ponderosa pine. You haul yourself up the penultimate quarter-mile by grabbing low-hanging branches, tree trunks, clumps of grass, anything that has a firmer grip in the ground than you do. When there is nothing to grab, you gouge your fingers into the mud, urging your slipping feet to follow suit. Then, suddenly you are there. On top of the world.

If it's midsummer, the first thing you notice are the ladybugs. They swarm everywhere, painting rocks and branches red, so dense you can hardly keep from crushing them underfoot. They take off from and land on your shirt so often that you feel like an international airport. The second thing you notice is that you are the tallest thing around with the exception of a pyramidal rock cairn some eight feet high. You are the tallest living thing, anyway—you and your companions dwarf the scrubby oaks that have a precarious foothold on the crumbling edges of the peak. The third thing you notice is that the surface of the peak is no larger than your living room. Five long strides would take you from one side to the other.

Dizzy with thin air and exhilaration, you find the trail register cached inside a metal ammo box and, with no small satisfaction, sign your name with the stubby pencil provided. You made it and your signature here proves it. The fourth thing you notice is that it doesn't matter. Size is relative. You may be the biggest thing on this oblong platform, but you feel like the tiniest object in the universe as the sky recedes rapidly in all directions. Who has conquered whom?

This is a good time to open your pack for a drink of water, a handful of trail mix. When breezes blow across your sweat-soaked shirt, raising goose bumps on your arms, you realize at last that you have indeed climbed out of the hot and dreary desert—and out of the claims and burdens of ordinary life, as well. You catch your breath at this astounding thought: for the next two days, you will be exactly where you want to be, doing exactly what you want to do. You are islanded, and no one and nothing can reach you. Then, your sense of proportion adjusted, you stand up—carefully, though, so as not to overbalance the peak and send it tumbling into the desert below—and take in your surroundings.

The view from Rincon Peak is endless—a hundred miles or more in every direction. You're an eagle, soaring over winding dirt roads, green pastures and tree-lined streams. With a few beats of your wings, you take in all of Southern Arizona, a vast pale plain ribbed with isolated blue mountain ranges—the Santa Catalinas, Pinaleños, Santa Ritas, Tucsons, Baboquivaris, Dragoons, Whetstones, Huachucas, Chiricahuas—a system of wales and furrows like corduroy, shape echoing shape as far as you can see.

This is the southern end of the Basin and Range Province, a territory not marked on any highway map. Geographers know it by the characteristic crest-and-trough landscape, a canvas painted with innumerable mountain ranges, some 10,000 feet or more high, their shoulders scraping the clouds, others low hills only a few thousand feet tall but with crests like broken ice, all separated from one another by miles of flatland or by tilted valleys known here by the lovely Spanish word *bajada*. These ranges and valleys formed under the dual forces of uplift and subsidence. Think of two blocks of wood side by side, then lower one and raise the other. The dropped block is the valley, the graben, geomorphologists call it, and the raised one, the horst, is the mountain range itself. They are often called mountain islands since the plants and animals that live on them are marooned by the surrounding desert or grassland as effectively as if they lived on real islands in the ocean.

I live in a valley, so mine is not an island life, but I have been on an oceanic island, and I remember what it's like. I could circle the island by car in a few hours. Whenever I looked outward, away from the island's center, my eyes fell upon ocean, miles of ocean, nothing but ocean, and I would remember that there was no escape but by plane or ship. This knowledge alternately exhilarated and depressed me. I wondered what it would be like to live there, to be unable to hop into my car and drive away— drive for hours or days out of one life and into another. Even though I never felt the need to do so in my mainland life, the knowledge that I could was somehow reassuring. For most of the plants and animals that live on mountain islands there is no way off at all; there is only the island life.

No two ranges in the Basin and Range Province are exactly alike; no two are completely different. The Santa Catalina and Rincon mountains, for instance, a pair of curving arms that enfold the Tucson basin in an unbroken line some fifty miles long, should be twins, since they were constructed from the same metamorphic rocks and subjected to the same climate and erosional forces, yet they could hardly look more different. The Rincon Mountains are smooth in outline, a hunk of kneaded clay. Their canyons are wide and shallow, open to view, hiding no secrets. The skyline of the Santa Catalina Mountains, in contrast, is infinitely varied and complex, an assemblage of peaks and ridges designed by different artists. The Catalina's canyons are shadowed, zigzag defiles. Despite these physical differences, the two ranges could hardly be more similar biologically. Ninety-five percent of the plants that grow in the Rincon Mountains also occur in the Catalinas, and similar belts of vegetation—successive bands of desert, woodland and forest—ring both. The animals repeat the pattern: in both you will find cactus wrens and coyotes among the ocotillos and cholla, rufous-sided towhees and chipmunks among the oaks, red-faced warblers and white-tailed deer with ponderosa pine and Douglas fir.

As you skip to other mountain islands, the biotic similarity with the Rincons trails off, but slowly, so that successive ranges seem to be blurrier and blurrier carbon copies. Even the Sierra Ancha more than a hundred miles to the north still shares 65 percent of its flora—some four hundred species—with the Rincon Mountains.

Thereby hangs a tale. For it isn't merely a hundred miles of distance that separates the two, it's a hundred miles of inhospitable desert interrupted by mountains, canyons, and rivers, not easy terrain for forest-dwelling plants and animals to cross.

So how *did* they get from one to the other? And, a corollary question, why is the vegetation and flora of these mountain islands so similar? Even so great an ecologist as Forrest Shreve, a gentle, perceptive, lanky man who spent the years between 1908 and 1915 exploring the Santa Catalina Mountains and nearby ranges, could not answer these questions with any certainty. He had ideas though.

His first explanation was almost too fantastic to believe. Perhaps climatic fluctuations had caused upward and downward movements of the forest and woodland belts on the mountain islands. During warm, dry periods, forest trees would have retreated to mountaintops where temperatures were lower and rainfall higher; during wet, cool periods, they would have crept downslope and even spread across the intervening valleys. "Such movements," wrote Shreve, "would alternately establish and break the connections between the vegetations of the various mountain ranges . . . thereby permitting the dispersal and subsequent isolation of species which might find no means of movement across the desert valleys under existing conditions." Unfortunately, he added, there seemed to be little or no evidence to support this intriguing idea.

The second possibility was that wind or birds might have transported seeds from one mountaintop to another. Like many another botanist before and since, he made lists: lists of plants common to the higher elevations of the Santa Catalina and the Pinaleño mountains, lists of plants found in one but not the other. But lists did not solve the problem, they only illustrated it. Next he collected seeds of plants that grew in the Pinaleños but not in the Catalinas and planted them in likely habitats in the latter. If they flourished, he reasoned, it would show that "their previous absence was due to their immobility" and would in turn suggest that long-distance dispersal, not wholesale movement of vegetation, had populated the mountaintops.

The seeds did not establish, and Shreve was left empty-handed since negative evidence proves nothing.

We might still be scratching our heads if not for the fortuitous discovery some three decades ago of fossilized packrat middens. Packrats, oversized mice that sometimes live in rock shelters, are compulsive accumulators, and their middens are junk heaps of everything they have ever scavenged—acorn caps, pine needles, snake vertebrae, cactus spines, bottle tops, bird bones, oak leaves. Because they never throw anything away, the midden heap keeps growing as successive packrats add to it. Their urine eventually cements the ragbag contents together, and, if the midden is well protected from the elements by a rock ledge, it can last tens of thousands of years.

If you scramble up a talus slope to a cave or shelter at the base of a cliff, peer inside and break off a hunk of a midden, you will readily notice its multiple layers. The darkest strata at the bottom, the oldest, are a rich, viscid-looking brown, the color of melting pine tar. Since desert plants like barrel cactus, creosote bush and paloverde dot the nearby slopes, you might be startled to see oak leaves and pinyon needles embedded in the matrix, especially as the nearest woodland trees are a mile or more upslope, far beyond the foraging range of the most active packrat. You might realize then that the surprisingly light, multilayered chunk of junk in your hand is actually a time capsule. Radiocarbon techniques, which can date its various layers with an accuracy of several hundred years, would show that the pine needles at the bottom of the midden were collected some thirty thousand years before the present when pinyon and scrub oak, not paloverde and creosote bush, grew near the midden shelter.

Packrat middens were the evidence that Forrest Shreve needed, but the discovery came after he died. Fossilized plant fragments from hundreds of middens across the Southwest demonstrate that the belts of forest and woodland on the larger mountains did indeed move up and down as the climate changed. Our mountains were not always islands. As recently as ten thousand years ago, they were joined by woodland instead of separated by desert, and forest-loving plants and animals could travel more readily from one to another. Because of this, anything you learn in one mountain island will probably apply to the others. All share a common stock of plants and animals; all share a common history.

Before I ever set foot in the Rincon Mountains, I spent several months in the herbarium preparing a preliminary list—a kind of proto-flora—of all the collections ever made in my study area. When hiking, I often brought it with me to make sure I wouldn't overlook species found many years earlier. I felt like a shopper in a supermarket as I crossed off Palmer's onion here and Griffith's sedum there, or searched high and low for lousewort, finally finding it in an unexpected place, as though it were a jar of marinated artichoke hearts shelved with fresh vegetables instead of canned.

I never did find everything on my shopping list. Some of these absentees were oddballs, like the cultivated barley collected long ago near the corral at Manning Camp, where some grains of horse feed had evidently germinated and grown to maturity. Exotics often appear for a season or two, then die out, so again I wasn't surprised when I failed to find black mustard or nit grass. But I *was* puzzled not to find wild rose in the aspen grove at Spud Rock Spring, where Jacob Blumer, a Swiss-born botanist, had collected it some seventy years before, and I was even more surprised not to find red osier dogwood along the creek below Manning Camp. The flora seemed to be changing before my eyes.

Hoping to locate roses and dogwoods somewhere, I devoted a few days to exploring out-of-the-way places like Spud Rock and Helen's Dome, oblong chunks of bedrock that thrust above the surrounding forest like fists, as hard and round as knuckles. I found neither wild rose nor red osier dogwood, but at Helen's Dome I stumbled across Rocky Mountain maple, a species that had not been collected in the Rincon Mountains since 1909, and shield fern, a prehistoric-looking plant with fronds as long as my forearm, another rediscovery.

Although I had often read about the importance of microhabitat for plants, I had never seen it demonstrated so dramatically. After nearly two years of walking trails without finding shield fern and Rocky Mountain maple, I had concluded that both were locally extinct. But all the time they were clinging to what must be their final outpost in the range. No doubt snow lingers on the deeply shaded slopes below Helen's Dome after it has melted elsewhere. This probably helps to keep the soil moist through the dry, hot months before the summer rains start. If not for Helen's Dome, Rocky Mountain maple and shield fern might well be extinct in the Rincon Mountains.

Search as I might, though, I never did find wild rose or red osier dogwood, and I finally decided that both must have died out, along with four other moisture-loving species Blumer collected that I couldn't relocate. All six doubtless depended on the winter snowpack to tide them over the arid foresummer. Several decade-long droughts since Blumer's day (including a series of exceptionally dry winters) were probably their demise.

These recent extirpations are analogous to a process that has been in operation ever since the mountain islands rose out of the desert sea. Every time the climate took a drier, warmer turn, forest and woodland plants retreated further upslope. The mountaintop patches of forest shrank like cotton cloth in hot water, with the result that some forest plants retreated off the mountain and out of existence. Because the Pinaleños are taller and more massive than the Santa Catalinas, they retained a larger patch of forest, therefore could support more forest-loving plants. This is one reason Shreve found certain montane wildflowers in the former but not in the latter, and why others, missing from the relatively diminutive Rincons, are abundant in the larger Santa Catalinas.

So floras change before our eyes and behind our backs. Species immigrate and become extinct; they dash up and down mountains like bighorn sheep. For this reason, scientists like to think of mountain islands as floristic experiments in the making. Shreve expressed the official viewpoint when he wrote that mountain islands "present innumerable phenomena of the greatest interest to both physiological and floristic plant geography and form a most fruitful field of investigation." I like to think of them in another way, too, as places where we can maroon ourselves—remote and islanded hideaways where, as Sarah Orne Jewett said, we can surrender ourselves to secret happiness.

Science with a Capital S

Science is built up with facts, as a house is
with stones. But a collection of facts is no more a
science than a heap of stones is a house.

While collecting plants, I have been stung by wasps, shocked by electric fences, rattled at by snakes, stabbed by cacti, mobbed by cattle, divebombed by blackbirds and gouged by barbed wire. I have lost my shoes in bottomless mud, sprained my ankle on two occasions and fallen into streams innumerable times. I have been honked at, hooted at and shot at. I've punctured tires and torn tie rods off trucks. It certainly doesn't look like science, yet much as fictional detectives are saddled with bumbling sidekicks, good biologists are not infrequently beset with minor calamity.

Perhaps the field scientist's cheerful willingness to risk injured dignity explains why the laboratory scientist distrusts her—a person who is scrabbling among rocks, tugging at the rhizomes of some recalcitrant grass while clasping her pen in her teeth and holding her field notebook under her chin doesn't look very scientific, whereas one pouring chemicals into test tubes does.

Laboratory scientists—and this includes physiologists as well as physicists and chemists—place their trust in the experimental method. They form an hypothesis, devise an experiment to test it, conduct the experiment and draw their conclusions from its results. This, to them, is real science, and any other method hardly deserves the name.

Field scientists seldom conduct experiments in this sense. You cannot manipulate the weather or a herd of elk in a laboratory—or outside of one, for that matter. About all you can do is form your hypothesis and attempt to disprove it with additional observations. Evolutionary ecologist Ernst Mayr calls this the observational-comparative method and emphasizes that, for biologists, it is as valid an approach as experimentation. "Observation in biology has probably produced more insights than all experiments combined," he says, a heartening assertion for those of us who feel claustrophobic when surrounded by test tubes, centrifuges and beakers.

If a scientist can operate largely by observation, what differentiates her from the observant hiker? Careful observers, after all, frequently see something worth noting as they stroll in the woods or across the fields: that Rocky Mountain maple and shield fern still grow in the Rincon Mountains, that acorn woodpeckers store acorns in the little holes they drill, that all the birds in a flock of gray-breasted jays help rear the young, that blue morning-glory flowers open at dawn and close a few hours later. The answer is that observations alone are not science. They must be tied to other observations, woven into an hypothesis or theory. An isolated observation is like an airmail postage stamp, a theory like the airplane that flies an entire cargo of mail. Only when observations are incorporated into the existing body of knowledge do they have any power to help us understand the workings of the natural world.

The observer graduates from natural history to science when her observations shape themselves as questions aimed at acquiring deeper insight. Which acorn woodpeckers in a flock accumulate the most acorns? Which are best at raiding another's stash? Do gray-breasted jays raise more nestlings to maturity than birds that don't cooperate with feeding chores? Are bees more attracted to morning glories than to flowers that stay open all day? Why should six unrelated species go extinct in the Rincon Mountains? Asking and answering such questions is the real work of science.

Whether done in the field or in the laboratory, by experiment or by observation, science is above all a conscious process. Making observations, forming an hypothesis, testing it, deciding that the hypothesis has been confirmed or falsified—none of this happens without full and deliberate attention. It's not like writing a story, where you sit with pen in hand and let the words pour onto the page from whatever overflowing source. It's more like writing a term paper for a history class. Expected to proceed in a logical fashion from point to point, you first prepare an outline of major topics and minor ones and guide your writing accordingly. The scientific method is the scientist's outline.

Scattershot science, where the scientist measures a group of variables, then tries to decide how they fit together and what they mean, takes a different approach. It ignores the outline and plunges happily to work, never enjoying itself so much as when it is puttering with tape measures, yardsticks and clipboards, like daddy in the garage on Saturday morning, putting nails in little jars, hanging hammers and pliers and wrenches from a pegboard, arranging cardboard boxes in nested stacks.

The lure of the measurable is hard to resist. Surely if you install enough rain gauges, hydrothermographs, anemometers, soil-moisture blocks and radiometers, run enough transects, map enough plots, it will all add up to something. The danger in taking the lure is not so much that you will be wasting your time as it is that, in the end, the urge to equate correlation with causation is as irresistible as was the urge to putter in the first place, and you find yourself concluding that the data you recorded caused the observations you made.

Sometimes, however, the scattershot approach is the best or even the only one. Chemists who search for biologically active chemicals in plants usually cannot predict which species will contain the most useful compounds. They can only screen plants more or less at random to see what turns up. Eighty years ago, Volney Spalding, an early plant ecologist, merely wanted to see what would turn up when he established nineteen permanent plots on Tumamoc Hill, an eight-hundred-acre desert preserve in Tucson. He marked the corners of his plots with rock cairns, then made a map of the vegetation inside each. This work was, he said at the time, "a debt to the future," since he would have to rely on unborn generations of ecologists to make his effort worthwhile. Forrest Shreve took up the challenge when he mapped the plots in 1928 and 1936, then later ecologists continued the task, until now Spalding's original quadrats are the longest-running permanent plots in ecological history. The insights these plots have produced far exceed Spalding's modest intentions and show that scattershot science sometimes hits a target squarely.

Compiling a flora is hit or miss, too. The goal is a complete plant list but from the beginning you know it is not attainable. Completeness depends on too many variables. You need good rains or you lose the species that remain dormant when it is too dry to suit their needs. You need frequent collecting trips or you miss the species that germinate, flower and die in a matter of weeks. You need a sharp eye to spot plants that are tiny or rare or otherwise hard to find. You must be willing to be uncomfortably dirty, hot and tired, and you must be physically fit. In the Rincon Mountains I learned all over again how difficult it is to collect plants when bone-tired from hours of plodding uphill in the sun. Just to unwrap the collecting bag, read the altimeter, make notes in my field notebook, and put the bag, altimeter and notebook away again took more strength than I had at times. I sometimes wondered how many plants went uncollected because I was too tired to see them. The network of trails was good, but even so, it left much territory uncovered. How many plants did I omit because they grew far away from any trail? The goal receded as fast as I pursued it.

Because of the scattershot approach, a flora can never be truly finished. It's like researching a biography. The accumulation of material—diaries, letters, memoranda, interviews, memoirs—could go on forever, but cannot be allowed to; when new information has finally slowed to a trickle, the biographer must call a halt and begin writing. After the book is published, a new letter will surface now and again, as will someone who knew the subject but was never interviewed, but this doesn't invalidate the principle, nor does it mean that the research was inadequate. The biographer can never know everything about her subject's life, after all; she can only hope to gather a representative sample of it.

A flora is likewise based on a sample. My preliminary list of five hundred species grew rapidly once I started collecting. At the end of the first year, I had added 120 names. After two years, the list had grown to 980. By that point, my sample of the flora was complete enough that I could find new species only by visiting out-of-the-way spots I had not seen yet, and even then, I wasn't assured of finding anything new. It was time to stop collecting and start writing.

After the flora was published, shoes began dropping left and right, as I had expected. Someone phoned to say that I had overlooked the maidenhair fern in an unnamed canyon off an unmapped trail. Someone else told me I had omitted the Douglas-fir mistletoe. A third person asked aghast, "No American spikenard? It's all over the top of the Catalinas." I shrugged my shoulders and made a note of my omissions; if I had collected for another two years, I would have slightly increased the size of my sample, but those shoes would still drop every once in a while.

Despite its inherent tendency to continue forever, compiling a flora need not be especially complicated or difficult. Even a botany student could have hiked the Rincon Mountains, collected the plants, identified them and assembled the names into a list. The job doesn't require forming and testing hypotheses, nor need it involve manipulation of data to derive mathematical models of how nature works. That's why some mathematically oriented ecologists, the ones who believe they have a monopoly on science with a capital "S," denigrate floras and other descriptive projects. Postage-stamp collecting, they call it, thinking, no doubt, of the birder's life-list, a cumulative record of every bird species the birder has ever seen.

The flora and the birder's life-list do seem remarkably similar at first glance. Are not both usually assembled by a single person? And aren't both lists of names? Yes, but. But the common thread uniting the many names on the birder's list is the birder herself. The names have no other logical and necessary relation to one another. The list is a personal one with only personal value. In contrast, the common thread uniting the names in a flora is the double-stranded one of place and time. Because the list permits comparison with other floras at other places and in other times, its value transcends the personal. A biological inventory as basic as the librarian's card catalogue, the flora is an invaluable tool for the resource manager, who must know what he has before he can manage it, and for conservationists, taxonomists, ecologists and anyone else who needs to know where certain plants occur. A flora is also a historical document, a snapshot in time. Using a good, "complete" flora as a baseline, botanists can tell which species have become locally extinct, which have recently appeared. Furthermore, until someone makes a point of thoroughly collecting an area, we don't know what unusual finds might lurk along little-traveled trails or in hard-to-reach canyon bottoms.

Descriptive work will always have a bigger role in science than some theoreticians want to admit. Certain geneticists, for example, are currently mapping the human genome, the complement of genes that determines our hair color, skull size, eye shape, propensity to inherit certain diseases and thousands of other traits. Although based on purely descriptive work, the genetic map will be of incalculable value in diagnosing and understanding heritable diseases, and, even more important, it will provide new leads and insights into research we cannot yet imagine. In the same way, floras can be used to explore a variety of questions. What do similarities and differences among a cluster of local floras tell us about the evolution of the landscape? What do they tell us about the conditions for species diversity? What can they say about changing climates, past and present? Floras provide clues to the history of the globe: Darwin used floristic information in formulating his theory of natural selection, and some of the earliest evidence for continental drift came from floristic work. As Jules Henri Poincaré pointed out, "Science is built up with facts, as a house is with stones." Floras are stones, and science is the house.

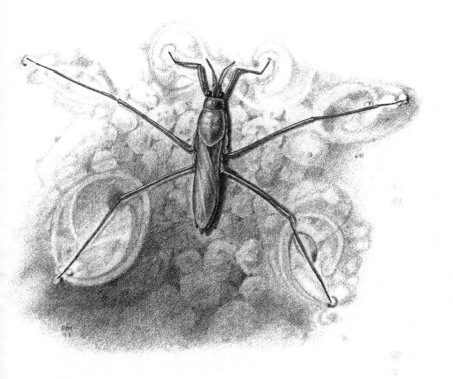

Words for Water

Until the Desert knows
That Water grows
His sands suffice
But let him once suspect
That Caspian fact
Sahara dies.

EMILY DICKINSON

We southwesterners need as many words for water as the Eskimos have for snow. There is winter water, icy clear from melting snow, and summer water, clotted with brown bubbles of algae. There is the dubious pink stuff that you would drink only as a last resort and the damp seeps no larger than a pocket handkerchief that only tiny wildflowers can use. Where ephemeral streams run over bedrock, water polishes the stone to marble smoothness. It hollows cavities where pools stare at the sky like unblinking black eyes; it carves sluices where the stream slips and slides, a thick, transparent cable. It trickles from pool to pool, one above the other like steps on a staircase, rattles down through rocky stretches, then suddenly sinks underground.

We need a musicology of water, too. Running water in the desert sings like water nowhere else. When I hiked in the Olympic Mountains, the thunder of one torrent had no sooner faded away than I could hear the muffled roar of another behind the next ridge. Desert streams make a subtler music. They don't roar, they tinkle, like ice cubes in a glass of tea, a liquid counterpoint to all the dry sounds of the desert—the beating of quail wings, the clacking of grasshoppers, the crunch of gravel underfoot. Long before desert hikers reach a stream, they find themselves anticipating the whisper of water on bedrock, and the anticipation is all the sweeter because desert streams are so transitory.

Water is life, we all know that; it is in deserts that we remember it, though. Where you find running water, you find hummocks of sedge flourishing in wet sand. Their long stems bend over the creek, a fountain of green. Nearby, tadpoles lie inert on olive-green sediments until you startle them, whereupon they shoot across the pool and dive headfirst into the bottom, sending up green mushroom clouds. Whirligig beetles spin madly as if afflicted with Saint Vitus's Dance, but they never collide. A garter snake oozes away between cattail stems. Except for the wiggling yellow stripe down its back, it's invisible against the black bottom of the pool.

The absence of water is death. Pools as they dry out smell like spoiled meat. Wasps seeking water step gingerly across the mats of algae, as delicate and fastidious as cats in wet grass. Sometimes they step too far and become mired in surface tension. Motionless water striders mass on the pool at its deepest end, their legs interlocked in a static web. If summer rains start soon, they'll survive; if not, their bodies will decay and contribute to the nutrient-rich powder that collects in the bottom of drying pools. Algae, insects, leaves, tadpoles: all must die and decay if the water dries up; all must abet the burgeoning life of sandy pool bottoms come the next rainy season.

I learned to cherish water in the Rincon Mountains because I couldn't take it for granted. Only a few springs were dependably wet year-round, and these were limited to the forest zone at the top. The other water sources—haphazard seeps, ephemeral streams and bedrock pools—were reliable during the spring snow melt and after heavy summer rains, but otherwise were catch as catch can.

When water is so rare, you want to interact with it. Hiking up the Manning Camp trail in midsummer, exhausted and irritated, blinded by my own sweat, barely moving through the hot, dense air, I kept myself going with thoughts of a certain secret stream-bed pool. The second I arrived, I would shrug off my pack and dump the collecting bags on the ground. Then I would strip off my wet clothes, spread them on the clean, flat bedrock, and finally slip with inordinate, exquisite relief into the cold, dark pool. Underwater my body was yellow and speckled with sediment stirred up from the bottom. There wasn't enough room to swim, but it didn't matter. It was enough to watch water reflections flicker on overhanging boulders, and to listen to dragonflies click as they zigzagged over the pool. When I was too chilled to stand it any longer, I would clamber out and pad around on the boulders, gripping the water-polished surface with my toes, enjoying the heat that an hour ago had seemed intolerable.

Little did I guess when I started the project that rattlesnakes and forest fires would be the least of my worries, while calculations about water would always loom large in my mind. Will there be any? Will it be safe to drink? Will there be enough? How much should I bring from home? Am I going to run out? Spilling a bottle of water could have meant disaster, so I always screwed the lids back onto my canteens before setting them on the ground, and I tried not to lose a single drop when pouring from the two-quart bottle into the hip flask.

My field notebooks mirror my obsession with water. Rarely, winter rains and melting snow made water a nuisance by its very abundance. "The stepping stones in Chimenea Creek were underwater today," I wrote on March 15, "and I had to take my boots off to wade across. The stream was icy, and I was thankful it was a narrow one." Usually, though, the problem was too little water. May 27 found me worrying along the Manning Camp trail that, because there had been so little rain, Madrona Creek would hold only bitter, black puddles unfit for drinking. "But just before I reach the canyon bottom," I noted, "I hear the reassuring rush of water." As I descended the Cow Head Saddle trail on July 4, I wrote, "Water scarce. Only a few greenish pools and no running water at all." At Happy Valley Saddle on September 6, I had expected to fill my canteens at the stream, "but instead of water I find a concentrated algal broth. Who knows whether it's potable or not? I decide to tough it out with the quart of water left in my canteen and make it back to the truck thirsty but with half a cup to spare."

A quart of water weighs two pounds, not an insignificant

figure when your fully loaded backpack already weighs thirty. Eventually I learned to calculate my water needs based on how much I was likely to find along the trail, which in turn depended on the season, but at the beginning I was like a pilot flying an experimental plane. I had to teach myself to learn.

My husband Steve accompanied me on many trips into the Rincon Mountains, partly out of botanical curiosity and partly to make certain I would come to no harm. But his knowledge of backpacking, acquired in the Pacific Northwest, proved close to useless in an arid climate. On our first backpacking trip into the Rincon Mountains, we each carried five quarts of water, ten pounds apiece, uncertain whether that would be enough but positive that neither one of us could carry another ounce. Starting in a waterless, cobbled stream bed, we soon climbed onto a low ridge and followed it through grassy, rolling foothills. From the trail we looked down onto the green river of treetops in Turkey Creek and up to the panorama of the Rincon Mountains where the massive Reef Rock floated like a steamship on a sea of forest.

The temperature most of the day was well over a hundred degrees, and the trail seemed close to vertical, so steep we would have been panting even if we hadn't been wearing heavy packs. Toward the end of the day we trudged twenty yards, then rested against trees or collapsed in the trail, trudged another twenty, then rested again. The worst of it, though, was our fear of running out of water. Every time I asked Steve for the canteen he carried on his hip belt, he watched me anxiously as I drank.

"Just a sip now," he would warn, and I would fill my mouth with water, swish it around, and finally let it dribble down my throat. But sips could not satisfy my craving for liquid nor moisten the dryness of my mouth. At times I felt like vomiting—a sure sign of dehydration—and only my reluctance to lose any more fluid than necessary prevented me.

By three o'clock we had been hiking for five hours and still had not arrived at Deer Head Spring. As we leaned against boulders in a shallow gully, I stared at the sandy ground, the lichen-splashed rocks, the trunks of oak saplings, and all seemed sinister and malicious, a Hobbity kind of forest with evil intentions. I didn't think I could go any farther. I was too tired, too thirsty, too sick. Steve, who was flushed and drenched with sweat, was silent. He looked so red I wondered if he was on the verge of heat stroke.

Those were the worst moments of the day. Of the entire project, in fact. If he had suggested we turn around then and go back to Tucson, I would have agreed. But he asked, "Ready?" and gave me a grim little smile, and we headed up the trail again.

By four o'clock, the air had cooled, and thirsty as we were, we felt better, felt that we were definitely going to make it. And then we lost our way where the trail had been destroyed by a forest fire some years ago. We looked at the map and saw where the trail was supposed to be, then looked at the landscape and saw a trackless forest of ponderosa pines and buckbrush. After we had thrashed around in thorny thickets for half an hour, watching the sun sink closer and closer to the ridge west of us, Steve cried, "Here's the trail, Jan, we've found it!"

We reached Deer Head Spring an hour later.

I'm no longer sure what we expected—perhaps one of those unsightly cement troughs that the National Forest Service calls a spring. Instead we saw untrammeled water, cold and clear and pure, flowing from a dry hillside where oaks and pines released a silent rain of leaves and needles. The first thing Steve did was fill two canteens. He handed one to me and I drank and drank and drank, water spilling down my throat, down my chin, down my shirt. I cupped my hands at the spring and the cold water welled up between my fingers and I splashed it on my face and poured it over my sweaty head and let it trickle down my back.

A park ranger had told me earlier that Deer Head Spring has the best water in the world. He did not exaggerate. Even now, Steve refers to the healing waters of Deer Head Spring, only half joking. A hydrologist would explain the spring as groundwater surfacing at a contact between colluvium and bedrock. But in truth, as I learned that day, a spring is a miracle, a promise, a renewal. How can we despair as long as Deer Head Spring flows quietly from pine needles and oak leaves, spills across rushes and sedges, grasses and violets, and rushes headlong and heedless into the forest below? It's the weeping eye that never ceases to weep, the heart that never fails to yield the lifeblood of the mountain. Deer Head Spring promises that we will never lack for water, nor for the things of the spirit—the deeper wisdom—that, welling up inside, nourish us and keep us alive.

The Cactus
and Other Anomalies

Sometimes I've believed as many as six
impossible things before breakfast.

LEWIS CARROLL

When I am away from the desert, I see it best. Otherwise, since it's all around me every day, my eyes refuse to take it in. My memory does a better job. I like to remember the desert as it appears in a rare spring, when brittlebush turns steep, rocky hillsides yellow, and the blue and orange of lupine and poppy speckle the gentler slopes. Less appealing but more enduring are memories of it in summer, when scorching cliffs match the fierce sunlight, and the brittlebush is cut to the bone, without flowers, without leaves, its white stems erect among blackened rocks. In summer the desert itself is cut to the bone. As the balmy warmth of April yields to the fatiguing heat of May, the saguaros wear garlands of white blossoms whose thick petals seem to have been molded in wax. By late May most of the spring wildflowers crunch underfoot like broken glass. In June the yellow blossoms of the creosote bush give way to fuzzy pods like spider egg cases that give the plants a dusty look, and the leaves of bursage shrivel on the stem, falling to the ground at the slightest touch. By July the saguaros are bloody-crowned, their ripe, red fruits split and dripping like axe wounds to the scalp. This desert of breath-stopping heat and vultures spiraling in a blank, blue sky is the real desert, the desert as it appears for six months of the year. The other is an *Arizona Highways* desert, one suitable for professional photographers and transplanted Iowans.

Paradoxically, some scientists will not admit that this territory is a desert at all. Too many trees, they say, too many shrubs, too much vegetation altogether. It must be thornscrub. Our paltry ten or twelve inches of yearly rainfall is excessive compared to real deserts, where it might not rain for a year, they point out. They use our cacti, virtual emblems of the desert, you might think, as evidence against us: the more desertlike the landscape, the fewer cacti you see, they say; therefore, by a topsy-turvy kind of logic, a landscape rich in cacti cannot really be a desert.

I wonder if they have ever been here in the summertime, if they have ever hiked down the Tanque Verde Ridge trail late in the afternoon as waves of heat rise from the rocks and the leaf-lets of mesquite and catclaw clamp shut against the heat. They would find that even the filigreed shade of a paloverde tree makes a welcome resting place then. Better still are the long columns of shade cast by saguaros where jackrabbits wait out the hottest part of the day. I did too, once. The shadow was just wide enough to hide my entire body from the sun when I sat on the ground, legs outstretched. Maybe these skeptics would convert when they discovered how the water in their canteens becomes so hot that drinking is a duty rather than a pleasure. Would they believe once they knew that a barrel cactus can survive for six years without water, without even having its roots in the soil?

This is true. Daniel T. MacDougal, a plant physiologist who came to the desert in 1906, excavated a barrel cactus, stuck it in an out-of-the-way corner of his laboratory and weighed it periodically to see how much water it had lost by transpiration. When he ended the experiment after six years, the weight had been reduced by a third, from eighty-three to fifty-five pounds. He didn't say whether or not his specimen bloomed. They will, though, as faithful to the time and season as the planets or the stars. I dug up a barrel cactus in my backyard once and set it aside, planning to resettle it when a likely spot became apparent. One never did, evidently, and I forgot about the plant completely until a year later, when it attracted my attention with five yellow flowers as bright as lemons.

For sheer water-holding capacity, the barrel cactus, which

actually looks less like a barrel than a pigeon-breasted matron, yields pride of place to the saguaro. Mature saguaros can grow to forty feet tall, produce a dozen arms and eventually weigh as much as six or seven tons, up to ninety percent of it water. The fluted stems swell during the rainy seasons, when the plants take up water from the soil, and shrink during droughts, when they metabolize the water they have stored.

I have lived in this desert twenty years now and should be so habituated to saguaros that I hardly notice them anymore. Instead, I find them as delightfully improbable as ever. A saguaro could be one of the six impossible things the White Queen believes before breakfast. All cacti have this air of improbability, as though nature threw up her hands and said, "Why not?" Why not eliminate leaves? Why not get rid of solid wood? What about a plant that's nothing but an oversized stem with some spines stuck on it here and there? We'll call it a cactus. Why not a cactus that is as tall as a tree and doesn't bloom until it's seventy-five-years old and lives for two hundred years? What about another with a root as big as a watermelon and sweet, white flowers that bloom only at night? And why not cacti that look like pipe organs or powder boxes or bowling balls? It's as though some mad engineer calculated every possible variation on a cylinder—stretching it, inflating it, squashing it, twisting it—and in doing so designed the entire cactus family.

The same engineer evidently lavished equal ingenuity on their spines, so much so that an experienced botanist can identify certain cacti from a cluster of spines alone. The spines of both the barrel cactus and the saguaro march up and down the plants in regular rows, but saguaro spines are straight as darning needles, barrel cactus spines curved like talons. The grizzly bear prickly pear takes its name from long, twisting spines so dense you can't see the pads underneath. Spines on the Engelmann prickly pear make a chicken-track pattern. The fishhook spines of the pincushion cactus are every bit as hard to disentangle from fingertips as genuine fishhooks.

So many desert plants poke and prod and prick you that your tendency at first is to call them all cacti and be done with them.

They are not, of course—the ocotillo with its long, gray wands and ephemeral leaves is not even a close relative, nor is the century plant, whose bayonet leaves bunch in a dense rosette. Both ocotillo and century plant have thorns, but thorns alone do not a cactus make. Only in cacti do the thorns—usually called spines— grow in clusters from circular areoles.

Their shared floral patterns is another reason cacti are grouped together. (Succulence, surprisingly enough, has nothing to do with it. Many different families contain fleshy plants.) All cacti have numerous colorful petals grading imperceptibly into less colorful sepals, numerous stamens thickly clustered around the pistil, and, above the ovary, a floral tube where nectar collects. In evolving to attract different kinds of pollinators, cactus flowers played multiple variations upon this basic theme. The yellow color, teacup shape, and abundant pollen of prickly pear flowers attract many kinds of bees and bee-flies. Claret-cups hedgehog is more exclusive. Its red, trumpet-shaped flowers appeal mostly to hummingbirds, and the nectar lies so deep within the tube that no bee can reach it. The white flowers of the saguaro, musky scented and placed high on the stem, probably evolved with bats as their main pollinators. Teddy-bear cholla, ironically named for the thick pelt of viciously barbed spines, gave up the dating game altogether. Insects seldom visit its inconspicuous, greenish flowers; instead, the plants reproduce mostly as fallen joints take root and grow into new plants.

As you might expect, cacti bloom improbably at the hottest, driest time of year when it hasn't rained for months and doesn't look like it remembers how. In late April and May, yellow flowers the size of teacups festoon the oval pads of prickly pear, a row of five or six blossoms that could have been stitched in place with the stiff, white spines. The staghorn cholla, branched like deer antlers, sports smaller flowers the color of dried blood. A wreath of crisp, pink flowers dwarfs the fist-sized pincushion cactus. (If saguaro flowers were as large in proportion to the stems, they would be the size of dinner plates; instead, they are only three or four inches broad.) All cacti bloom every year without fail, no matter how dry the winter or how hot the spring.

The flowering of cacti at the start of summer—or the end of spring, however you want to look at it—is one of the few dependable events in the unpredictable desert. Given this un-predictability—sparse and irregular rainfall, blistering summers, freezing winters, no two years the same—cacti do not seem quite so unlikely. In fact, they make perfect sense. The variety of cac-tus shapes represents multiple solutions to the general problem of staying alive and the specific problems of staying alive in the desert. Saguaros, the cactus version of a tree, branch as they age, eventually producing a candelabra of arms. The more arms they have, the greater their surface area, and the more surface area they have, the more food they can manufacture. Prickly pears, the cactus counterpart of shrubs, accomplish the same goal by producing more pads, stacking them one on top of the other like the spinning dinner plates in a juggling act.

As with most solutions, theirs involve compromises. Succu-lence, their signal characteristic, enables them to survive lengthy droughts but leaves them vulnerable to frost damage when ice crystals form inside the tissues, rupturing and destroying the cells. The great size of the saguaro, combined with its shallow roots, makes it susceptible to wind throw. Toppling in storms is not a problem for the sprawling prickly pears, but being a poten-tial moisture source for thirsty desert creatures is. Give and take, action and reaction—evolution is an iterative process, and few choices are free of consequences.

I never did collect a saguaro, although, theoretically, every plant on my final list should be represented by a voucher speci-men. The theory, a good one, is that only a properly pressed, mounted and labeled specimen on file at the herbarium is proof positive that saguaro—or any other plant—occurs in the Rincon Mountains. A plant specimen can always be reexamined, and therein lies its value. A published statement cannot be dissected under a microscope. As so often happens, however, theory ran aground against practicality—and there's nothing practical about pressing a saguaro.

How would you do it? Very carefully, if at all. Obviously,

there's no hope of folding it accordion style, the way you would a cattail, until it fits inside your press. A saguaro specimen, therefore, usually consists of a flower or two and a strip of skin with spines attached; thus do botanists reduce this noble plant to its taxonomic essence. Even the smaller cacti make forbidding specimens, requiring slicing and salting and many changes of blotter to draw out their moisture. Every time you handle a prickly-pear specimen, a few more spines anchor themselves in your fingertips and the fine barbs called glochids drift onto your face where they sting like slivers of glass. It's enough to make you think that spines are the cactus's solution to the problem of being collected by botanists.

Spines certainly seem as though they must be a solution to something—an adaptation, in evolutionary terms. Because they are so menacing to us thin-skinned humans, we tend to assume they evolved to protect the fleshy cactus from hungry or thirsty animals. Unfortunately, this hypothesis, attractive as it is, doesn't work. Coyotes, desert tortoises, javelinas and ground squirrels greedily devour the sweet, succulent fruits of prickly pears without regard to the glochids. You would think it would be like chewing a mouthful of needles, but they don't mind. Even the much stronger, stiffer spines on prickly pear pads do not discourage a determined javelina; in the dry season the scalloped pads show where these wild pigs have munched away regardless of the two-inch-long thorns. As the great desert ecologist Forrest Shreve once said, "The spines are no sharper than their hunger."

Science has yet to definitively explain why cactus spines exist, but it has come up with some good possibilities. Using computers, plant physiologist Park Nobel and his colleagues compared normal spiny cacti with hypothetical spineless ones. They found that spines, by shading the stems, prevent heat damage to the tissues during the hottest summer days. Spines also change the circulation of air next to the cactus, helping prevent frost damage on the coldest winter nights. Once spines evolved, they may have kept some animals from champing succulent cactus tissues, but this would have been, by and large, a happy accident. We should keep in mind, too, that the earliest cacti were leafy, tropical plants with slender, woody stems and weak spines that served no obvious function. Spininess is built into the genetic blueprint of cacti, just as fingernails are built into the human one.

Figuring out adaptations is a tricky business, fraught with pitfalls for the evolutionary biologist. We speak loosely of cacti as being adapted to the desert, for example, when the very phrase is so broad it is almost meaningless. To be precise, we should say that certain features ensure their survival in deserts. Absence of leaves, those water-hungry, drought susceptible, all-too-edible appendages, is one. The waxy coating that prevents water loss through joints and pads is another. So are the enlarged stems that permit storage of enough water to tide the plants over droughts of months, even years.

Despite these apparently desert-adaptive features, most experts agree that cacti evolved not in the desert but in thornforest, a deciduous woodland where crowded trees scratch and claw at passers-by. The remarkable succulence of the cactus, it is said, may serve other purposes besides coping with drought—an extended growing period, for one. The reasoning is this: Cacti can extract water only from wet soils, and in thornforest, soils are wet only after rains. The slow-growing cactus *should* be at a disadvantage, since the more rapidly growing trees would quickly deplete the soil moisture, leaving none for the cactus to grow on. But, since cacti are succulent, they can take up water from rain-wet soils and save it for later. This stored water lets them grow for months after the soil dries out, so they aren't at a disadvantage after all.

Millions of years after the first cacti evolved in thornforest, the regional climate became warmer and drier. As deserts spread across the landscape, cacti found themselves preadapted to conditions that many of their associates could not tolerate. Their succulence and spininess proved beneficial in unexpected ways, and before they knew it, they had become emblems of the desert.

All life is a concession to the improbable, says a character in a Norman Douglas novel. The cactus family has not so much conceded the improbable as fostered it.

The Land of Oaks

Who wants to understand the poem
Must go to the land of poetry.

JOHANN WOLFGANG VON GOETHE

Where is the poet who will sing the beauty of our evergreen oaks? There is silverleaf oak with willowlike leaves dark green above and white beneath. When the wind blows, the white side flashes in the sun, reminding me always of fairy-tale trees hung with leaves of real silver. There is netleaf oak, with tough, pliant leaves that turn maroon, the color and texture of fine morocco leather; scrub oak, with plump acorns borne cap to cap, noses pointing in opposite directions like Doctor Dolittle's pushmi-pullyu; Emory oak with shiny green leaves the size of postage stamps, sharply toothed like Christmas holly. All share the unmistakable oak silhouette, trees daubed in oil paints, the foliage thickly laid on in blocks, the trunks and branches roughly sketched with a dry brush. At its lower edge, oak woodland is scrawny and dwarfed. Ancient trees may be no larger than children. But as you climb through the woodland, the oaks gradually increase in stature until you find yourself in a forest where oak leaves pad the ground, a parti-colored carpet of umber, dove gray, silver and cinnamon.

If you walked through oak woodland in April or May, you might think you were following hard on the footsteps of a bad fire. More leaves lie on the ground than hang from the trees, and the few still attached are gold or brown or copper or beige. Why should they be called *live* oaks you wonder. Underfoot, the thick leaf carpet crunches and crackles. The woodland has a dusty and unfinished look, as though someone had started to sketch in the trees, then gave up. It seems unnaturally bright—all that unaccustomed sunlight flooding through the twiggy canopies—yet you will not find much in flower, not like you would in a spring woodland in New England. The checkered trunks are bright with lichens, though, orange, mint green and yellow, and a broad-billed hummingbird, gorget flashing in the sun, adds a touch of red as he hurtles between the trees.

Although the oaks are losing their leaves, spring isn't a resting time for them. Winter is over at last—no more danger of frost for another eight months—and the soil is still moist from winter rains and snow. In another month or two, the days will be quite warm, even hot, and the earth will be parched. Now, in these brief weeks when water and warmth coincide, the oaks must simultaneously shed the trappings of the last eleven months and prepare for the next eleven. Tiny new leaves unfurl on bare branches, and a few trees, freshly green, look scrubbed and bright.

One spring, hoping to refurbish my dwindling compost pile, I went to the woodland with a generous supply of plastic trash bags and collected enough leaves to fill the back of my pickup truck. Bag by bag I turned them into the compost heap, watered them well and waited. And waited and waited. Week after week, as I turned and watered the pile, I watched coffee grounds, watermelon rinds, paper towels, banana peels, avocado pits and grass clippings disintegrate, decay and disappear, but the oak leaves persisted. Other than turning black, they hardly changed at all. After six months I was still waiting.

Oak leaves here are meant to last. In New England, where winters are severe, oaks and other deciduous trees shed their leaves as a matter of survival. In the Southwest, however, oak leaves stay on the tree all year because winters in oak woodland, while chilly, are not especially severe. It's a rare day when the temperature doesn't rise above freezing, and minimums much below zero degrees are unheard of. Many days are positively balmy, warm enough for plants to carry on photosynthesis, and by retaining their leaves all winter long, oaks can manufacture food when the opportunity arises. There's no point in letting all that good sunshine go to waste. While their tough, leathery leaves show that evergreen oaks are adapted for hot, dry weather, they can't take too much of it. All along the lower edge of the oak woodland, where the trees thin out and grasses, century plants and cacti take over, you can see standing skeletons of oaks, dead for twenty years and more. The drought of the 1950s, when winter precipitation fell far below normal for eight years in a row, killed them. And while our evergreen oaks look very pretty as the first snow of winter sifts onto the leaves and stripes the trunks, they cannot handle too much snow either. One spring I arrived in pine and oak forest near the top of the Rincon Mountains to find that as many as a third of the oaks had broken in half. Jagged branches dangled from splintered trunks, and tree tops rested on the ground. Dead leaves still clung to the twigs. Evidently, an extraordinarily bad winter storm had deposited so much snow that the oaks had collapsed. Their blocky canopies are not well suited for shedding snow, unlike the conical ones of pine and fir. Our evergreen oaks exist at the fulcrum of a climatic see-saw, sensitive to drought and heat at one end and to cold and snow at the other.

Oak woodland is a lively place, not solemn and damping to the spirits like the dense fir forests above, nor enervating and overly quiet like the sunstruck desert below. Often I saw deer, especially in burned areas, where they browse the fresh green foliage sprouting from blackened trunks. Once I crept close enough to see their limpid eyes and the tawny fuzz on their antlers and to hear the muffled snap of twigs being torn from branches. I saw skunks, too, unmistakable white streaks undulating over rocks and logs in the half-light between sunset and night. Comically clumsy, absurdly terrifying, they scurry about the woodland floor, noses to the ground, searching for insects, lizards, eggs, bones, fungi and any other edible scraps. Oblivious to hand claps, shouts and outright threats, one blundered right up to me as I lay in my sleeping bag, and only veered off when I raised up suddenly on my elbows.

One lazy afternoon, replete with collecting yet not tired enough to nap, I sat under an Arizona oak and let the woodland world come to me. Black pinacate beetles trundled across the leaf litter, hind ends poked into the air. Horse lubbers—giant black grasshoppers veined with green—crashed about in the undergrowth. California sisters—wide-winged, brown butterflies splotched with orange and white—glided in and out of the sunlight. A bridled titmouse, its ferocious black eyebrows like a Samurai warrior's, scolded me as long as I sat there. Overhead, an ash-throated flycatcher perched on the outer twigs of the oak and periodically swooped after flying insects. If I listened carefully, I could hear its bill click with each catch. Scuttering in the dead leaves rufous-sided towhees made as much noise as bears. A flock of gray-breasted jays played follow-the-leader, bouncing from branch to branch and yelling imprecations. I had not sat there too long before the jays approached me one by one in a hopeful fashion, respectful yet self-assured. When I tossed one jay a piece of cracker, he scratched a hole in the ground with his bill, then buried the tidbit for later consumption.

Dozens, probably hundreds, of lives unfolded around me, and the oak was the center of them all. Feeders on oak foliage, the caterpillars of the California sister are so cleverly disguised that I have never found one, but the bridled titmouse that gleans insects from the twigs and leaves of oak trees no doubt discovers them all the time. Both she and the ash-throated flycatcher nest in holes in oaks, and the gray-breasted jays construct their nests in the leafy canopies.

Of all these creatures, it is the gray-breasted jay that is most inseparably wedded to oak woodland, where it is a year-round resident. Each flock jointly occupies and defends a territory, about two acres of woodland, which successive generations inherit in turn. Not only do jays nest amid oak foliage, they depend on acorns for half their diet and find the rest—insects and miscellaneous seeds—by tossing aside dead oak leaves with their strong bills. Jays bury acorns for later retrieval, inadvertently planting woodlands wherever they go, avian Johnny Appleseeds.

In all these details, the jay defines itself as something more than the taxonomist's *Aphelocoma ultramarina*. It is the sum of its activities, and everything it does—the food it eats, the habitats it selects, the way it secures a mate, the enemies it escapes—are part of this larger identity: its niche, as ecologists say.

If oaks are crucial to the survival of gray-breasted jays, these raucous birds are equally critical for the perpetuation of oaks, since acorns will not germinate until they are buried. Jays are, therefore, an important aspect of the oak niche, a niche being everything a plant or animal does. Oaks are pollinated as wind blows pollen from male to female catkins, another aspect of the oak niche. So is the loss of leaves at flowering, which permits pollen to drift more freely from one canopy to another, and the nearly evergreen habit that allows manufacture of food almost throughout the year. Rainfall requirements also define plant niches. If an Emory oak is to produce a bumper crop of acorns in the fall, it must have had at least fifteen inches of rain the preceding winter, and, if the acorns from that crop are to germinate, they require at least ten inches of rain the following summer.

Once you know what to look for, you notice niches as well as individuals. You see, too, how niches intersect, like those of oak and jay. This is the way ecologists see plants and animals—less as separate entities than as communities of interacting organisms, an infinitely reticulating web that covers the surface of the globe. We have long understood in a philosophical sense that all living creatures are somehow interconnected. Now we know it is a biological truth as well.

Demolition Derby

I take infinite pains to know all the phenomena
of the spring, for instance, thinking that I have
here the entire poem, and then, to my chagrin, I
hear that it is but an imperfect copy that I possess
and have read, that my ancestors have torn out
many of the first leaves and grandest passages,
and mutilated it in many places.

HENRY DAVID THOREAU

A saguaro begins to bloom before it develops the whorl of arms that make it seem so human. Each arm can produce up to one hundred flowers in a season, and each flower can generate more than two hundred seeds. That is 200,000 seeds each year for an unbranched plant and a possible 30 million seeds over its 150-year lifespan. You might think, therefore, that saguaros should stand shoulder to shoulder, arm to arm, across the desert. Not so long ago they nearly did. Photographs of Saguaro National Monument taken in the 1930s show a veritable forest of the giant cacti at the base of Tanque Verde Ridge. In fact, the monument was established mainly for their sake. Now, however, the cactus forest is sadly depleted. Only one out of three saguaros from the thirties remains.

In some ways, the saguaro is its own worst enemy. Since they're usually the tallest objects around, they're magnets for lightning during electrical storms. When struck, they explode on the spot. Saguaro roots radiate from the plant for yards but lie only a few inches below the soil surface. Although admirably adapted for absorbing the lightest rains, shallow roots are not an effective anchor for a thirty-foot pillar, and when the soil is wet, strong winds send the giants crashing to the ground. The force of their fall is so great that their trunks split open and their massive arms shatter.

Sorry to say, humans are sometimes a far worse enemy. Greedy cactus collectors dig up and sell plants of portable size, although this has been illegal since 1929. Vandals throw rocks and bottles at the trunks, admittedly a tempting target, yet the holes they make will always remain as ugly pits and scars. Malicious curiosity leads others to push the giant cacti over, destroying in a matter of minutes the endurance of two hundred years. People subject saguaros to multiple smaller indignities: festoon them with colored Christmas lights or hang tires over the arms as though these magnificent plants were yoked oxen to be driven at one's bidding. Some years ago, a man trying to shoot off one of the massive arms was killed when it fell on him. I don't know anyone who mourned the passing of this yahoo or regretted the macabre manner of his demise. Usually, though, saguaros do not fight back; they suffer in vegetative silence when felled by bulldozers for housing developments or riddled with buckshot by drunken cowboys. Anglos could take a page from the book of the Tohono O'odham, the Papago Indians who have lived in this desert for centuries. The saguaros are like men, the Tohono O'odham teach their children, and to injure one is to hurt another human being.

These are only a few of the many ills saguaro flesh is heir to. Most of every seed crop is eaten by birds, javelinas, mice, packrats, ants and coyotes. The few seedlings that do emerge are liable to be gnawed off at the ground by thirsty rabbits and rodents before they reach an inch in height. The small plants that manage to escape the dinner hour may freeze to death in exceptionally cold winters unless well protected by overhanging trees or shrubbery. During the days when cattle grazed in the monument, many small saguaros must have been trampled underfoot, too. For these and possibly other reasons, saguaros at the monument seemed to be on their way out, since, as old plants died, there weren't enough young ones to replace them.

This is one conservation story that should have a happy ending, however. In the last two decades, hundreds upon hundreds of seedling saguaros have sprouted in the former saguaro forest. Because they grow with almost infinite slowness, they're all quite small—some the size of tennis balls, many no larger than marbles—and they don't show up in landscape photographs yet. But if we can wait another hundred years, the bajada at Tanque Verde Ridge may look as it once did, crowded with sentries striding across the hills in seven-league boots.

Other changes, wrought by humans, have not reversed so handily and perhaps never will. The Mexican gray wolf once roamed the Rincon Mountains, but it has been hunted almost to extinction there and throughout the state. From 1870 to about 1910, long before Saguaro National Monument existed, a limestone kiln near the present-day visitor center required abundant firewood for extracting lime from the rock. The trees closest to hand, mesquites and paloverdes, although scrawny, were certainly abundant, or at least they were until the kiln operators began cutting them. It's thought that decimation of these trees contributed to the eventual decline of saguaros, since the seedling cacti thrive best in the shelter of mesquites and paloverdes.

Even after the monument was established in 1933, ranchers continued to run cattle there as they had for fifty years, and, as everywhere these bulky marauders roam, disruption followed. The abundant prickly pears on the gentle slopes, so thick you cannot walk a straight line in many places, are a legacy of cattle ranching. Cows wouldn't eat them, so the cacti multiplied beyond any reasonable or attractive level. They became weeds, plants out of place and out of control. As cattle trampled and devoured their way across the gentler slopes, the original grasses and wildflowers disappeared to be replaced by weedy shrubs that, like prickly pears, increase under heavy grazing. Now, fifteen years after cattle were kicked off the monument for good, the vegetation shows little sign of recovery. To the uneducated eye, the landscape looks ordinary enough, but to someone who knows, it's a war zone after the peace treaty has been signed.

It seems that humans are incapable of settling anywhere without playing demolition derby with the landscape. Other organisms can adapt or expand their niches to a limited extent, as do the jays that beg for crackers or the poinsettias that naturalize along Hawaiian roadsides, but only humans undertake wholesale manipulation of their niche. Because we make our own micro-climates, we can survive in places otherwise inimical to human life—the Antarctic, the ocean floor, the moon. We developed agriculture and irrigation, assuring a constant food supply. We cleared forests for farms, denuded grasslands for livestock. We tended to see every creature that didn't directly contribute to our welfare as vermin and undertook pest control.

Until now, evolution has consistently favored this short-term outlook. The need for food is immediate, intense. If the easiest and most efficient way to feed ourselves and our families is to drive an entire herd of buffalo off a cliff, so be it. We don't foresee that eventually the buffalo population will dwindle to the verge of extinction. We require shelter, too. Cutting pine trees to supply roof beams for our enormous, populous pueblo, we find that we must go further and further afield to find suitable timber, and if eventually we have cut away the entire forest and as a result the soil erodes so rapidly that agriculture is no longer possible, how could we have anticipated that? The solution, inconvenient but not impossible, is to move on. Other forests await.

The paradox is that if we were not shortsighted, we probably would not have survived, yet now this very trait, which has proved so adaptive in the past, threatens our continued existence. Anyone with eyes and lungs knows this, and knows, too, the painful necessity of contributing to the very pollution that overwhelms us all. We worry about the effect of smog on our health, but we don't give up our automobiles. We worry about the sheer bulk of garbage we produce as we continue to produce more. Our collective guilt is even greater. Our indispensable monocultures of corn and wheat demand heavy use of toxic chemicals that accumulate in rivers and lakes. The plume of sulfur dioxide that flows downwind from smelter stacks poisons all the vegetation in its path, yet, because profit is king according to our shortsighted way of thinking, the copper companies pollute without restraint.

Our shortsightedness threatens the existence of the countless organisms who share this planet with us. Every summer, fewer hermit thrushes return to the eastern United States because clearing of the Brazilian rain forest for ranching and mining has decimated their wintering grounds. Our ill-advised attempt to control coyotes and mountain lions in northern Arizona resulted in such multiplication of deer that thousands starved. When niches collide instead of overlap, it is invariably the humans who win. Too often I turn away from this planet's pain. When worried voices on the radio start telling me about disappearing rain forests, dying cypress swamps, polluted tidal marshes, I flick the knob to another station, reluctant to accept their portrait of a shattered world. A newspaper photograph of an oil-sodden gull, the whole intricate mechanism of barbule and rachis now fouled and useless, cannot be forgotten once seen, and I rapidly turn the page. Hawaiian rain forests stocked with houseplants gone wild, a florist's shop turned inside out; sand dune lizards literally deafened by the roar of all-terrain cycles; Mayan temples dissolving in acid rain; remote portions of the High Sierra suffering under the well-meaning onslaught of thousands of wilderness lovers— I see no place on earth where I can escape.

Is there no solution? Three million years of evolution for shortsightedness weigh against one. The mamo, a nectar-feeding bird of the Hawaiian rain forest, was driven to extinction by loss of habitat and will never return. The last living panda will die in a zoo, the last Hohokam agave in an arboretum. The automobile will outlive them both. We have outfoxed ourselves, we all-too-clever humans, with our internal combustion machines, our trichloroethylenes and dieldrins, our invincible shortsightedness. As a human being, I still hope, but as a biologist I fear.

Thomas Gray Was Wrong

Full many a flower is born to blush unseen, and
waste its sweetness on the desert air.

THOMAS GRAY

The North Slope trail in the Rincon Mountains passes first through an open forest of ponderosa pines that look like bottle-brushes with long, red handles, then through denser Douglas firs, their lower branches bare of needles but shaggy with lichens, and finally through white firs so closely spaced that the forest absorbs all light, just as the rotted needles underfoot absorb all sound. In the pine forest, natural clearings turn into small meadows where clones of silvery sneezeweed shine in the sunlight, but in the white-fir forest, the only clearing is the trail, a path of light two feet wide and a hundred feet high.

Voices sound unnaturally loud, ringing through the forest, so you tend to speak in low tones. The air is moist, you can feel it in your lungs, a kind of pulmonary fog. Once the summer rains have started, clouds brood over the mountain for days at a time, and then there really is fog, sizzling droplets that make you want to wipe your eyes so you can see better. The unaccustomed chill makes you glad for sweaters and woolly caps and gloves.

On other days, summer storms build gradually from clear, sunny mornings. Thunderheads loom up behind the ridges, mass overhead, darken, then rage, releasing at last the tension and foreboding you have felt all day. Waves of rain press wildflowers to the ground. Pine needles thrash in the wind. Bolts of light-ning strike and strike again, and you remember how a lightning-struck pine looks, stripped to the bare blonde wood, a charred furrow spiraling down its trunk.

After one such storm, I emerged with relief from my humid tent. On the mountain I felt closer to storms than I did in the city, more vulnerable to their power, and I was always glad to have survived another one. It was good then to sit on the sloping bedrock beside Manning Pond and watch the evening close in. Violet-green swallows whirled in the sky, their bellies flashing white in the last bars of sunlight. One by one they swooped down to the pond to drink, hardly pausing as they dipped and soared. I heard whirring behind me and turned in time to see a hummingbird at the red flowers of a hedgehog cactus. As she thrust her bill deep into the flower's tube, her head disappeared among the petals, and the enormous red mouth of the blossom seemed about to swallow her.

Along the North Slope trail the next morning, water ran everywhere. The mountaintop leaked like a sponge, as though it had soaked up all the rainfall it could, and, unable to hold any more, dribbled from every pore. Wildflowers abounded in the forest that summer, and I rejoiced in being a botanist. My special knowledge made me feel less of an intruder. Walking the North Slope trail, I brushed among flowers as dense as in a garden: wands of red-flowered penstemon, fragrant white clusters of boneweed, pink and white daisies on thick leafy stems. Bumblebees fumbled at the flowers, which plunged to the ground under their weight. The wet meadow at Spud Rock Spring was lush with the varied greens of sedges, grasses, and rushes, an enormous lawn spread like a picnic blanket among the pines and aspens. Purple blossoms of blue-eyed grass dotted the meadow in their thousands. I wept with pleasure for a childhood dream come true. The dry meadows were verdant, too, junglelike in their profusion of bracken fern and cut-leaf coneflower, all growing six feet tall. As I followed the overgrown trail through the forest of herbs, I felt like a dwarf, or a cartoon character dropped into a fantasy world where everything is four times its normal size.

One July day I made fifty collections and only stopped because I had finally run out of plastic bags. In the pine forest I found puccoon, with yellow flowers like miniature trumpets and stems indelibly stained purple at the base; mock pennyroyal, among whose tiny lavender flowers big, black carpenter bees bumped and browsed; a vining pea, which clambered over shrubs, its purple flowers perched like tiny butterflies along the twigs. Real butterflies flickered overhead or alit with delicate touch on the flat, yellow heads of sneezeweed. Hummingbirds probed the orange tubes of Arizona honeysuckle, suckling its honey.

The pale ghostly blossoms of the fir forest were subdued in comparison to the pine forest flowers: in shades of white they gleamed against the duff, a quiet signal for the inconspicuous flies and bees that inhabit this denser forest. And this, after all, is the point of flowers: not to please botanists, but to signal pollinators.

Thomas Gray, you see, was wrong. Flowers seldom waste their sweetness on the desert air, or on the forest air, either. Their fragrance, color, shape and size are a code that tells potential pollinators what they have to offer and who should expect to earn it, like Victorians for whom red roses meant, "I love you," and purple pansies said, "You occupy my thoughts." In the condensed language of flowers, the red color, tubular shape and turned-back petals of scarlet penstemon announce a hummingbird flower. Many insects cannot see red, so they tend to ignore red flowers. In this and several other ways, scarlet penstemon is specialized *for* hummingbirds and *against* other visitors, particularly bees, which might try to steal the nectar without carrying away any pollen. Wild verbena, with its dense, flat-topped clusters of pink or lavender flowers and delicious sweet scent, calls to butterflies. The purpled blues of lupine signal bees, the only insects adept enough to work the complicated blossoms. And, of course, there are the innumerable, ubiquitous, yellow flowers, the Esperanto of the insect world. Most yellow flowers, especially the sunflower types, attempt to attract pollinators in general rather than a specific type of pollinator, and innumerable visitors can reap their pollen and nectar rewards.

Some pollination mechanisms seem better designed to stretch

our credulity than achieve pollination. A common Algerian orchid lures male wasps by imitating in color, pattern and aroma the female wasp. In attempting to copulate with his sham partner, the wasp pollinates the flower. The Australian triggerplant, like some kind of vaudeville comic, unexpectedly slaps its bee pollinators on the back with a bag of pollen. "Trap blossoms" like the arum lily use an irresistible stench to lure flies to a chamber at the base of the flower, then imprison them for a day. After the fly escapes, well-dusted with pollen, it stupidly repeats the process in another flower, depositing its pollen load upon the stigmas.

I have never seen a wasp mate with an orchid, but I have watched small wild bees clutch the anthers of senna flowers and make a loud buzz—a shrill, tight spiral of sound like a dentist's drill—to vibrate pollen grains out of the anther tips. I have, in fact, spent hours crouched over flowers and insects, a gigantic voyeur from another world. Inside the collapsed flowers of wild gourds, I've found squash bees, large golden-brown bees with long spiderlike legs and enormous eyes, fast asleep. They had been up before dawn to pollinate the flowers, which, like squash blossoms everywhere, are early risers. I once saw a hawkmoth, a stubby body and blur of wings, hover at the white bowl of an evening primrose. As it slipped its needle of a tongue into the nectar tube, its head plunged deeper and deeper into the blossom's throat, and for a second or two its wings ceased beating as it rested motionless on the lowermost petal. I have never tired of seeing midnight-blue butterflies alight on lavender thistles and deftly uncoil their threadlike tongues into the capillary flowers, nor of watching bees plop into the forest of stamens inside a prickly pear flower, disappear into the wriggling mass and emerge a minute later drenched in pollen.

Some day I hope to see hawkmoths at sacred datura. The extravagantly large trumpet flowers open at dusk, a moonlike white in the dim light, and wilt by midmorning of the next day. The nectar accumulates in narrow channels deep within the flower's throat. According to Verne Grant, who has studied the matter, hawkmoths turn drunkards at sacred datura. His dry, precise language barely masking his glee, Grant wrote that the moths "were clumsy in landing on the flowers and often missed their target and fell into the leaves or onto the ground. They were slow and awkward in picking themselves up again. When they resumed flight, their movements were erratic as if they were dizzy." Imagine what Emily Dickinson would have made of this: the little tipplers who, inebriate of air, taste a liquor never brewed. Evidently, the alkaloids that make all parts of sacred datura fatally toxic to humans have a less virulent effect on the moths. In fact, according to Grant, "they seem to like it and come back for more." Who wouldn't? Debauchees of dew, indeed.

I'm a flower watcher everywhere I go. On vacation in southern Utah, my husband and I stopped along a highway to botanize in a huge, sloping meadow where pale blue irises speckled a tight, green sod of grass, sedge and rush. Buttercups glistened wherever trickling water moistened the soil. Willows here and there turned silvery as the breeze ruffled their leaves. Swallowtail butterflies lofted on air currents, then veered to right or left, as agile as Japanese fighting kites. Broad-tailed hummingbirds whizzed and whistled around us. Their flight lines, if made visible, would have fenced us in like crisscrossing wires. As a female hovered at an iris flower, a male rushed at her, chittering, then spiraled into the sky. Climbing straight toward the sun, he paused for half a second, then plummeted like a roller coaster, pulling up at the last moment.

"Well, I'm impressed," Steve said, and I agreed that if I were the female hummer, I'd capitulate.

We watched the meadow until our legs were tired of standing, then we sat down and watched some more. And to think we almost passed it by, we said afterwards. There was no highway sign advertising so esoteric a roadside attraction, of course, not even a proper turnout for our car—a far cry from Disneyland, where little plaques show where to stand to take your souvenir snapshots. To be a naturalist is to discover your own roadside attractions. In that meadow, with its willow islands and profusion of blue iris and yellow buttercups, we found scenery as beautiful as in any national park, yet we had the entire place to ourselves. If it had been a national park, dozens of cars would have filled a paved parking lot, and crowds of people would have already chased the hummingbirds away. More than that, we ourselves would have approached the scene with different attitudes. We would automatically have expected our experience to be beautiful, unusual or instructive, since our national parks and monuments in the West are, of course, all of these. And as we walked the trails and read the interpretive literature, we would have found ourselves donning a kind of zoo mentality, as though all this had been laid on especially for our entertainment and edification. I am unendingly grateful for our national parks. I wouldn't wish any one of them to be a single acre smaller. But the fact remains that merely delineating a piece of ground and calling it a national park subtly changes our attitude toward it. We begin to believe that the land is special because it's a national park, not the other way around. Like Thomas Gray, we tend to believe that beauty is beauty only if we are present to witness it and only if the experts have already placed their stamp of approval on it.

The corollary is that we fail to realize how special our ordinary world really is. We come to national parks and other preserves primed for appreciation yet disdain the fat, maroon caterpillars on the pipevine in the alley or the mockingbird on the clothesline with an earwig in its bill. Thoreau said, "I had no idea that there was so much going on in Heywood's meadow." Heywood's meadow is all around us.

PART III / THE WORLD BEYOND

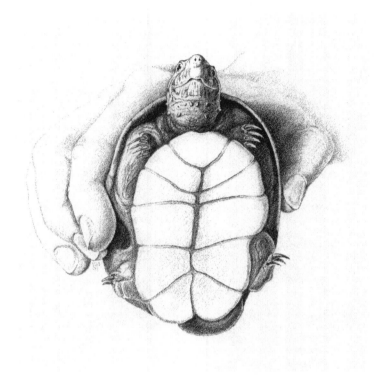

The Blessings of
Wilderness

The real blessings of life are not the fictions
generally supposed, but are real, and are mostly
within reach of all.   WALT WHITMAN

I

Humans have been ever ready to bend wilderness to their own
purposes—burning prairies for game, clear-cutting forests for
timber, damming rivers for electricity. I see a difference in degree
but not in kind between the man who builds a dam and the one
who expects wilderness to be his psychiatrist.

The idea that wilderness can transform us beyond recognition
—or at least reconcile us to our shabby, unregenerate selves—is
one of the curious myths of our times. Strange, how we expect
nature to do for us what we cannot do for ourselves. We expect instant change, like instant soup, and the recipe is as clear as
the directions printed on the back of a package of Lipton's: take
to the woods, for only in wilderness can you grow, as Thoreau
said, like corn in the night.

The summer I worked at Canyon de Chelly National Monument in northeastern Arizona should, by all rights, have been
just such a time of growth and transformation. I saw things that
summer I had never seen before, ordinary events to some but
miracles to a child of the suburbs. Safe in a rock shelter one
hundred feet above the canyon floor, I watched a thunderstorm
march through the gorge. High overhead, water streamed down
the cliffs and fell in front of the shelter like a curtain of twisting glass beads. It drummed on the rocks below like hundreds
of stamping feet. The dull red sandstone gleamed as rain slicked
its surface. Far below, running water in the stream bed gathered

momentum and became a white-capped wave surging down the wash. Thunder echoed up and down the canyon, reverberating against the cliffs as lightning flashed over the pinyons on the opposite plateau.

On fine days, I would stand near the head of the canyon in the late afternoon and watch hundreds of violet-green swallows wheeling overhead. In swift pursuit of flying insects, they rifled by my head as though they would drill a hole through my skull. I found broken pieces of Indian pottery scattered on the ground among the pinyons and sagebrush. Some were earth-red, with thumbprints impressed in rows like a crimped pie crust; others were boldly painted with ocher and rust and ebony or finely hachured with black lines on a white slip.

Watered by permanent streams, deeply cut into red and buff sandstone, the monument's three canyons are sinuous, with flat, sandy bottoms and perpendicular walls honeycombed by caves and overhanging rock shelters. Our work involved climbing from the canyon floor into the caves and shelters to look for artifacts left by the Indians who had lived there centuries before—crumbling stone walls still chinked with mud, mortars and pestles, thumb-sized corncobs, fragments of sandal plaited from reed, and paintings of men, goats, lizards and hands on every smooth rock surface.

Often we climbed via ancient Indian trails whose innocuous names—Baby Trail, Bear Trail, Woman Trail, Many Ladders Trail—belied their danger and the skill needed to traverse them. Some ascended cliffs by means of ladders that were no more than notched logs half-rotted from exposure to sun and rain. Others climbed by toe- and hand-holds carved into the rock, little cups just big enough to contain the toe of your boot, stone pockets polished smooth by countless feet and hands.

Before every climb—and we climbed almost weekly—I secretly vomited, so great was my apprehension. Afterwards, safely back on the ground again, I was too shaky to eat for hours. I froze on Bear Trail once. Halfway up the trail I found I could go neither up nor down. I could only crouch on a knob of rock that hung far above the canyon bottom. For five minutes, legs trembling, arms quivering, fingertips pressed so tightly against the rock they ached for days afterwards, I waited for death or deliverance. The latter finally arrived in the form of a crew member who asked, "Need some help?" then held out his hand to steady me as I placed one foot after the other in the toe-holds and climbed up and over the knob.

This simple act of kindness was uncharacteristic. Mostly the men on the crew taunted me, the kind of teasing that cuts like paper. "You did that pretty well—for a girl," they would say after I successfully climbed a tricky pitch. In this way, even small triumphs took on the color of failure. Never had I felt so ashamed of the way I was.

Midway through the summer, as a kind of self-imposed rite of passage, I went alone into Canyon de Chelly on an overnight hike. I borrowed a rucksack, filled it with a sleeping bag, a canteen of water, some crackers and salami, and set off.

My plan was to hike down Red Clay Canyon to the bottom of Canyon de Chelly, walk down-canyon about four miles and hike back out via Black Rock trail. Early on, I came to a fifty-foot cliff, but could not find a safe passageway down to the terrace below. Looking in my pack to consult my map, I discovered that I had left it behind. Should I go back? I wavered, then decided to go on: I would rather travel blind than turn back defeated at the start. After an hour of nervous searching back and forth across the lip of the cliff, I finally discovered the downward trail and reached Canyon de Chelly late in the afternoon. Strolling along the sandy creek bed, watching the stream slip by, I began to think about my route back, at first idly, then with something approaching panic. Without my map, how would I know which side drainage held Black Rock trail? And which way was it from here, down the main canyon or up? I could not remember.

Thunderheads had been gathering all afternoon, and while I hesitated, a few drops of rain spattered on my arms. Turning my back on Canyon de Chelly, I headed back the way I had come. As the rain thickened, I took shelter in a shallow cave as long as my body and just wide enough to keep me dry.

By the time the storm rolled away, it was nearly dark. I made myself as comfortable as possible on the uneven cave floor, wedging my body between blocks of sandstone which had fallen from its roof. Lying in the dark, I listened to sand trickle down the walls and wondered if this was the night another block would work loose.

In the glad light of morning, I walked back out, back up Red Clay Canyon, back up the fifty-foot cliff, back to camp.

In retrospect, it seems that the trip was not so much a rite of passage as a rite of confusion. Who did I think I was? What did I think I was doing? Did I expect a vision? I no longer know. If all I wanted was to prove I could spend a night alone out-of-doors, I succeeded. But if I expected to return utterly changed—self-reliant, wilderness-wise, fearless—I failed. A rite of passage marks a change: change cannot be forced by the performance of a rite or by the simple expedient of taking to the woods.

2

In those days I believed, as I had read in books, that wilderness simplifies the complexities of our lives. I no longer find that to be true. In the Rincon Mountain wilderness I never did learn how to reconcile the child's thrill at stumbling upon a rare plant, the scientist's need to explain its presence in a particular spot, the mystic's impulse to drop to my knees and meditate upon it, the collector's ferment that pushed me in search of further stimulations. After one trip I wrote in my field notebook, "Too much to do, and all at once. How can I rest in a meadow after a six-mile hike, collect all the plants that have flowered since my last visit, take the photographs that show both the beauty and the plant ecology, make the necessary notes, recharge my body with water and food, and converse with my companions?" Wilderness, I learned, is infinitely complex, a bewildering and ultimately ungraspable mixture of thoughts, sights and sensations.

I am not an expert on wilderness. I am not even certain what that would involve: it's like claiming to be an expert on God. But I have known some of her blessings.

An encounter with a bear in the Santa Rita Mountains near

Tucson was one. Perhaps because the day was hot and muggy and fur coats were the last thing on my mind, I didn't expect any bears. But as I sat under the oaks with my lunch, bright blue moths sprayed up from nearby bracken fern, and I caught sight of something large and brown that had scattered them. A cow, that was my first thought, but then, not twenty feet away, the furry snout appeared from behind the bracken, and the massive head turned towards me and stared.

Hypnotized, I stared back, and I memorized as many details as I could—the rich red brown of his fur, his liquid black eyes, his ponderous body, his nostrils sniffing in my direction, the sunlight shining through the bracken, the moths dancing overhead, his complete absence of fear.

I, on the other hand, while not frightened, was uncomfortably aware that temptation was spread all around me in the form of crackers, salami, cheese and apples. For what seemed like long minutes I sat without moving, as this wild creature gazed at me and I at him. My leg, cocked beneath me, prickled, but I wouldn't risk shifting my weight. I scarcely breathed. I had no idea what was going to happen next.

This was the blessing. Not to know. To have no script, to be at the mercy of wild chance. The bear eventually lumbered away, leaving me with the realization that we are always at the mercy of wild chance. Nothing is predictable except that life will end, but we forget. Living our scheduled, structured days we become too safe, we live in the middle. Wilderness puts us back on the edge.

One evening at dusk, high-pitched, musical whistles echoed high above my forest camp on the Mogollon Rim in central Arizona. I thought it must be a bird and imagined, from the volume of the cries, a Russian firebird swooping over the pines and crying its ineffable song. I thought of it as a huge, long-tailed creature with an elegant crest and ruffled, red plumage spangled with silver and gold. The following morning, the cries had degenerated into shrill calls, many voices at once, and I thought instead of a flock of big birds—sandhill cranes or herons. I walked down a dirt road toward the source of the noise and saw what appeared to be a flock of wild turkeys at the far side of a meadow. I polished my glasses, walked a little closer, and the screeching turkeys transformed themselves into bawling elk.

As I stood there, transfixed, one jumped the barbed wire fence and paused on the road not twenty feet in front of me. Several more quickly joined it, including a calf that ran like a puppy after the others as they headed across the road and into the forest. Back in the meadow, a mob of fifty elk, mostly cows and calves, milled on the other side of the fence. When they finally saw me, they bolted, crying and squealing as they hurtled to safety. Then the elk who had crossed the road returned one by one, jumping the fence with fluid grace, and the entire herd thundered across the meadow and disappeared among the pines.

It took me a while to catch my breath after that, but not long enough. As soon as I returned to camp, I recorded it all in my field notebook. Already the experience had become a trophy, the kind of story we tell for self-aggrandizement. At the moment it happened, though, it was pure. This is another blessing of wilderness—to experience without thought of profit or advantage.

Over a long summer weekend in the Rincon Mountains, it rained enough to set the streams in motion, and going down the mountain I found running water and pools where I had seen dry sand four days before. It was probably the rain that brought the Sonoran mud turtle out of its summer slumber. When I first saw the turtle, it was swimming in a shallow pool, and it tried to hide by sitting motionless in plain view. I picked it out of the water to get a better look. Fleshy, pointed warts roughened its neck and tail, and the top of its shell, not much larger than the palm of my hand, was blotched with rust-colored rectangles. Underneath it was yellow. The turtle reeked, an odor like dirty socks or spoiled meat, no doubt a deterrent to potential predators. This didn't deter me, however, and I held it for a few minutes, the slick shell wet against my palm, the little feet scrabbling against my hand, when suddenly I shuddered with the realization that this was no toy, no pet. This was a living being I had no right to touch.

It reminded me of the time when, driving south on Country Club Boulevard in Tucson, I saw a child peddling down the street ahead of me on her tricycle. I slammed on my brakes, plucked her out of the road, returned her with ill-suppressed tears and indignation to her unconcerned parents. For hours afterwards I felt the solidity of her squirming body against my chest, the wispiness of her hair against my chin, things I had no right to experience. What lingered was the strangeness of holding a child who did not belong to me.

So often we stride through the world, thoughtlessly claiming it as our own. It is good for us to feel that we have no right. This is another blessing of wilderness—to remind us that we intrude.

We go into wilderness expecting one kind of magic; with any luck, we find another kind altogether. Anyone who walks in the wild will discover the untamed edges of life; anyone who spends time in wilderness will, at times, feel like an intruder. Walt Whitman told one of his beloved soldier-boys that "The real blessings of life are not the fictions generally supposed, but are real, and are mostly within reach of all." The blessings of wilderness are also real and are mostly within reach of all.

Seeing Truly

Our meddling intellect
Mis-shapes the beauteous forms of things.
WILLIAM WORDSWORTH

Twenty years ago or more, I sat on a rock in a stream for a good fifteen minutes, waiting for *it* to happen. Water tumbled around me, spitting into the air and spinning around the rock. Cottonwood leaves shivered overhead, flicking shadows on my skin. I stared at the water, which was wet, and at the sky, which was blue, but nothing happened. I kept thinking about my husband, studying at home, and about a chemistry final I should have been studying for myself. I thought about the hole in the side of my tennis shoe and how shoes didn't last the way they used to. I thought about lunch—was there still a can of tuna in the cupboard or should I stop by the store on my way home?

Finally I gave up. *It*, whatever it was, obviously wasn't going to happen to me. The situation reminded me of the night when, as a high school freshman, I read Mary McCarthy's *The Group* under the covers by flashlight. By the time I came up for air, she had convinced me not only that any female can have an orgasm but that she should have one the very first time. The McCarthy Syndrome is what my girlfriends and I called it when we eventually discovered that the real world seldom mimics fiction.

There by the stream it was the Annie Dillard Syndrome that had struck. Having read her *Pilgrim at Tinker Creek* three or four times, having loved it so well I underlined many passages and learned a few of them by heart, I wanted to experience nature the way she did: "I filled up like a new wineskin. I breathed an air like light; I saw a light like water. I was the lip of a fountain the creek filled forever; I was ether, the leaf in the zephyr; I was flesh-flake, feather, bone."

This kind of intensity comes more naturally to some people than others. I'll never forget sitting with a friend on a rock ledge that overlooked the Grand Canyon. The view was one I had seen so many times on postcards and calendars I could hardly take it in: the cavernous space that fills the immense gorge; the canyon walls a layer cake of lavender and purple and blue; the gnarled and sturdy pinyons hanging by one arm and leg from the cliffs— all this seemed less real than the idle thoughts banging around inside my head. I thought about one of the other members of our little group: was he attracted to me? I thought about my sun-burned shoulders and neck and decided that I would definitely wear sunscreen the next day. I wondered if we would have fried potatoes for breakfast again.

Meanwhile, night closed in on the canyon. A lavender haze blurred the opposite cliffs, and a sliver of a moon shone brighter and brighter in the deepening sky. People traveled halfway around the world to gaze at that scene, and all I could see was a Sierra Club Calendar. February or March, probably. I very nearly said, "Ho hum, just another fabulous view of one hundred million years of earth history." Fortunately, I didn't, for when I turned toward my companion, I saw that he, overwhelmed by beauty, wept quietly.

This silenced me. It silenced my tongue, that is, for it seemed that nothing could calm my brain, which rambled on inanely about hamburgers and clean socks, as irrelevant and irreverent as a ticker-tape machine at a wedding.

We can try to invoke the deliberate, delicate attention that lets us see truly, but, as Annie Dillard points out, we aren't likely to be successful. I have felt it descend on me at unexpected times— when sketching, say, or moving to music—and I know now how it feels: a mantle of awareness enveloping my mind the way sleep overtakes me as I drowse in bed. To become aware of my aware-ness is to lose it, however: self-consciousness not only spoils the effect, it is utterly foreign to it, by definition inimical.

Are poets any more successful at invoking their muse? I suspect they pray, "Sing heavenly Muse," as Homer did, then settle for the usual—a day or two of blinding inspiration, many more of dutiful plodding. Of course, they have it backwards: the muse of poetry or dance or awareness comes from the inside out, not the other way around. The muse is a metaphor for the times when we transcend ourselves, and so is the awareness we find when we see truly.

With a guilty conscience I realize how little time I took to really observe when I was collecting in the Rincon Mountains. Observation seemed to conflict directly with assembling the flora, two different brain modes, perhaps; I calculated rather than appreciated, worked rather than played. Seeing—truly taking in one's surroundings—means, for me, sitting. And more than sitting, it means sitting and looking and listening and, above all, turning off the constant chatter in my mind. Collecting means keeping on the move, and keeping up as well a constant internal conversation: did I get that plant yet, do I want to get this one, have I put that one on my list, is this a different species of grama grass, am I going to run out of bags, if I have this from Douglas Spring do I need to collect it at Colossal Cave?

Time is the crucial element here. If I feel hurried or harried, the muse keeps her own counsel. But if I make time—not a grudging minute or two, but hour upon hour uncongested by duties, tasks and lists—she might settle in my heart for a while.

One memorable backpacking trip into the Mogollon Mountains of southwestern New Mexico gave me just this kind of time—or, more accurately, forced it on me. Since I was on vacation, I had no appointments, schedules or deadlines and could linger where I pleased. For once I had time enough to sit without moving until the forest forgot my presence and carried on its life around me. A fox with a small animal dangling from its mouth crossed the creek on stepping stones. Pygmy nuthatches combed the trunks of pine trees for bugs. A pair of squawking Steller's jays flew in checkerboard progression from one tree to another as they made their raucous way downstream. Minute creatures took on an interest and importance they had never had for me before. Sitting on a boulder above a stream-bed pool, I saw a spider spinning its web in the water, or thought I did, until I altered the focus of my eyes and saw it dancing in the air between the stiff leaves of a sedge. I made a game out of discovering the cleverly concealed caddisfly larvae—bits of twig or scraps of leaf that weren't twigs or leaves at all but tiny, shrimplike insects swaddled in camouflage. So still did I sit that a butterfly perched beside me and sipped the sweat from my socks, which I had spread on a rock to dry. It had as much time as I did, all the time in the world. Time hung like trout in the stream.

Yet even then, I never lost consciousness of myself. Years of scientific training made that impossible even before I set foot on the trail. The butterfly, a California sister, I sketched for later identification. I scribbled a query about the caddisfly larvae in my field notebook: does a given species consistently use only grass or gravel for its case or does it employ whatever materials are handy? While I wanted to feel at one with the natural world, another organism among millions, my compulsion to collect and analyze set up a barrier, turning my interaction with nature into one of observer and observed. Science imposes a schizophrenic split upon biologists. We may want to feel part of the natural world, and for a time we may imagine we are, but we must always retreat if we are to write science, not myth.

Ways of seeing become ways of knowing. How you choose to see the natural world depends on what you want to know about it, and what you know is conditioned by how you have seen. Study nature, not books, exhorted the great naturalist Louis Agassiz. Thoreau would have agreed. "It is only when we forget all our learning that we begin to know," he wrote in his journal. "I do not get nearer by a hair's breadth to any natural object so long as I presume that I have an introduction to it from some learned man. . . . If you would make acquaintance with the ferns you must forget your botany. You must get rid of what is commonly called *knowledge* of them. Not a single scientific term or distinction is the least to the purpose, for you would fain perceive something, and you must approach the object totally unprejudiced."

This, to Thoreau, was seeing truly. To a scientist—Thoreau's much-despised "learned man"—seeing truly is something altogether different. A pair of gopher snakes performs a subtle dance, first gliding side by side, then entwining, but before they finish their performance, something frightens them off. What have we seen—a courtship ritual or a territorial display? Totally unprejudiced though we might be, having forgotten, as Thoreau advised, our herpetology, we might welcome the commentary of a learned man or woman. A bee returns to her hive and crawls about for a moment before she disappears into the pulsating throng. This is all we would notice but for Karl von Frisch, whose painstaking research decoded the bee's behavior, so that we now recognize her seemingly random movements as a precise description of a new food source.

Sight and knowledge interact. Together they are an iterative process, a system of input and feedback. You see, you learn, and learning more, you see better.

Poet Marge Piercy knows this. "In the natural landscape, you don't begin to observe until you have some vocabulary, some set of criteria to apply, some kind of grids to put down," she writes. "People who have never done bird watching at all don't know what birds look like. They have no way of looking at the different kinds of birds that are in their landscape or what they are doing there. To understand why a warbler has one kind of beak and a finch has another kind of beak. Why the different kinds of ways of flying happen: the darting flight, the soaring flight, the hovering flight."

When a botanist looks at an unknown plant, her brain processes dozens of bits of information, often without her conscious knowledge. This is the grid of which Piercy speaks. Stems square or round? Leaves opposite or alternate? Flowers borne in spikes, racemes, umbels, thyrses or corymbs? Petals four, five, six, ten, numerous? How many stamens? Do the crushed leaves smell minty, skunky, camphorous? Having processed these and other clues, she announces, "*Artemisia ludoviciana,*" or "A mint," or "Obviously Umbelliferae, but I don't know the genus."

Toward the end of his life, Thoreau came around more and more to the biologist's way of seeing. Some readers prefer the strident philosophizing of the earlier Thoreau. Odell Shepard, who edited a collection of the journals, wrote that in the last few years of his life Thoreau filled hundreds of pages "with minute notations of things measured and counted, mostly written in the lifeless style of professional scientists against which he had so often railed."

But a person grows as he must, and Thoreau grew out of his philosophizing into the wider world of observation, induction and experiment—in a word, science. In 1852 he began assembling data for his "kalendar," a detailed account of the comings and goings of plants and animals in and around Concord. He systematically listed all the trees, flowers and ferns in the area and noted when they leafed, bloomed and fruited. He noted the arrivals and departures of birds, measured the water level in rivers and ponds, recorded the daily weather. These observations culminated in huge charts on which he listed the natural events of every day through nine annual cycles.

He distrusted his own data gathering, though, and maintained a paradoxically disdainful attitude toward science and its productions. "I must walk more with free senses," he abjured himself. "It is as bad to *study* stars and clouds as flowers and stones. I must let my senses wander as my thoughts, my eyes see without looking." He wanted his kalendar of Concord to be something more than a phenological document, something more than mere science.

What he sought was a way of knowing, and all he knew was that science would be antithetical to it. "How little I know of that *arbor-vitae* when I have learned only what science can tell me!" he told his journal. "There are twenty words for the tree and its different parts which the Indians gave, and which are not in our botanies, which imply a more practical and vital science. He was well acquainted with its wood, and its bark, and its leaves. No science does more than arrange what knowledge we have of any class of objects."

The biology of his day was indeed, as he complained, largely a matter of classification and taxonomy, as was appropriate for a country so recently settled and inadequately explored. Perhaps modern-day ecology, with its emphasis on interactions and concepts, would have pleased him better. In his work on the kalendar, he struggled toward the kind of knowledge that unifies diverse bits of information, yet he could not surrender himself completely to what he understood as the sterile viewpoint of a scientist. He wanted something deeper, more nourishing. He wanted to penetrate beyond science to a place that science could not apprehend.

He yearned for ultimate understanding, for the burst of insight that ties everything together. Like Edna St. Vincent Millay, he might have cried, "O world I cannot hold thee close enough." None of us can, no matter how many collections we amass, no matter how many notes we take. Science, as Thoreau realized, cannot deliver this kind of understanding, nor is that its function. The ultimate eluded Thoreau, as it eludes us. This is just as well. Ultimates, pinned down on paper, reduce themselves to nothing, not like a sauce reduced to its essence but like water boiled out of a pan until not even a film of moisture remains.

The Great Paper Memory

What a richly colored strong warm coat
is woven when love is the warp and work is the woof.

MARGE PIERCY

I love the homely, matter-of-fact titles of scientific articles: "Chromosome Number in Some Cacti of Western North America," "A New *Encelia* from Baja California," "Seedcrop Characteristics and Minimum Reproductive Size of Organ Pipe Cactus in Southern Arizona." What you see is what you get. Each is a precise description containing enough information so that a reader, scanning a bibliography, could decide whether a particular title was worth pursuing further.

A scientific title does not necessarily convey its meaning to everyone, however. Flipping through back issues of *Science*, I cannot make heads or tails of some: "GaAs Clusters in the Quantum Size Regime: Growth on High Surface Area Silica by Molecular Beam Epitaxy," or "Malondialdehyde-Altered Protein Occurs in Atheroma of Watanabe Heritable Hyperlipidemic Rabbits." With effort, I can figure out the gist of some, much as a child, learning to read, sounds out unfamiliar words. It's not that I am stupid; presumably a solid-state chemist would be as baffled by a title like "Mycorrhizae Associated with an Invasion of *Erechtites glomerata*," as I am by his on clusters in the quantum size regime.

No matter who your audience is, when you publish a piece of research, you contribute knowledge that did not exist before, and that's a worthwhile accomplishment. Unless you are at the top of your field, though, you will be lucky if anyone other than your spouse or your office mate knows about it. One hundred sixty-five thousand titles are published in biology each year in about nine thousand different journals. Scientific publications—books, articles, monographs, and so on—double in number every ten to fourteen years. In some fields they increase even faster than that. Any single paper, therefore, has as much chance of making an impact as a stone dropped off a pier has of raising sea level. In fact, two sociologists suggested that the average scientific paper—indeed the average scientist—is so much filler, like the tidbits of information once used to pad out newspaper columns.

One reason scientific papers proliferate as mindlessly as yeast cells in a batch of bread dough is that too many scientists are careerists first and seekers of the truth second. Their publication record helps them find jobs, receive promotions, get fellowships and grants. The more publications they have, the more productive and valuable they appear. Some scientists, therefore, publish the same piece of research in two or three different journals, and others make several short papers out of what should have been a single long one. This isn't exactly fraud, but it's not exactly legitimate either, and the result is to clog our informational channels with disinformation.

None of this affects me directly. It's the careerist rats who are threading the mazes, pushing the levers, running the treadmills. Since I don't have a doctorate, I'm not even part of the experiment. There's no pressure on me to publish or perish, or to accumulate a publication record of five hundred papers. It affects me indirectly, though. I must wear blinders if I am to operate as a scientist. I can't tell myself, "You might as well drop pebbles into the ocean for all the difference this is going to make," or I'll go crazy. All I can do is carry on with the work I love, knowing that it makes a difference to me and hoping that this will, finally, be enough.

A scientist has two obligations to the literature of science: to contribute to it and to read it. Reading not only prepares and stimulates the mind, it also keeps scientists from reinventing the wheel or the autoclave and ensures that they will give credit where it's due. As the great entomologist and ecologist William Morton Wheeler wrote, "Whenever one does decide to publish it is necessary to reckon with the great 'paper memory of mankind' . . . if only for the purpose of bringing the new work into intelligible, organic relation with the old." Failure to do this, he said, "may be justly interpreted as carelessness, sloth, ignorance or conceit."

The sheer volume of literature makes it difficult for scientists to live up to this obligation, however. Knowledge is growing infinitely faster than our ability to keep up with it, so we become stupider day by day. It's possible to keep abreast of developments in your own field in the past five years, more difficult to spread your net over the two decades before that, and nearly impossible to take into account all work of possible relevance that was done more than thirty or forty years ago. Two ecologists I know spent hours measuring the diameters of saguaros (the trunks, pleated like accordions, swell and contract as they take up and lose water), not realizing that Effie Spalding had beaten them to it by eighty years.

I'm not at all surprised that they weren't aware of her research: not only was it ancient history, ecologically speaking, but she published it in an obscure journal and—most important of all— no one had cited it in the intervening period. The best-known papers of whatever vintage are referred to again and again in the literature, which makes them clearly visible and ever more likely to be cited. Seldom-cited papers suffer the opposite outcome, and—unless fate intervenes—eventually fade into total invisibility.

Over the years, the significance of a piece of research inexorably changes. What was a brilliant discovery at the time, a seminal contribution, eventually becomes a name and a date inside the shelter of a pair of parentheses. It loses its impact as a stimulant and becomes a historical footnote. The more remote a piece of work in time, the more apt it is to be submerged by recent research. By this unfortunate but inevitable process, ordinary scientists are forgotten, their papers no longer read or cited, their key discoveries attributed to later researchers.

The great paper memory is a faulty one.

I first learned of one such forgotten scientist from herbarium specimens, several hundred collected in the Rincon Mountains in 1909. The petals had mostly faded to the color of a tea-stain, but otherwise the specimens, having been well-made to start with, were in good shape. "Plants of the Rincon Mountains, J. C. Blumer, Collector," read each label. Underneath, the plant name, collection number, date and location were written by hand in tiny script.

You do not learn much about a person from his herbarium specimens. I was curious enough that I went to some trouble to dig up as much information about Blumer as I could find. Eventually, I published a bare-bones sketch of his life and work, thereby putting myself in the position of writing a paper only a few people would read about a character everyone had already forgotten. When Jacob Blumer moved to Arizona from the Midwest in 1906, he was thirty-four and had a bachelor's degree in botany from Iowa State College. Hoping to earn a living by selling specimens, he collected in the Chiricahua Mountains in southeastern Arizona for two years. Then, while briefly employed as a research assistant at the old Desert Laboratory in Tucson, he mapped the distribution of ten thousand saguaros on Tumamoc Hill and environs, a task that must have been tedious beyond description. He apparently spent the years from 1909 to 1912 collecting here and there in Southern Arizona, including a summer and fall in the Rincon Mountains, then went to Canada, where he worked as a forester. In 1917, he made one last attempt to earn a living by collecting and selling Arizona plant specimens, but soon gave up. He told an acquaintance, "I shall probably go farming on my brother's land, which is more patriotic as well as more remunerative at the present juncture than botanizing. Those of us botanists who are not so fortunate as to draw steady salaries are made poor by our hobbies. And yet the hobby is sometimes life itself." He spent the rest of his life on the family farm in Minnesota. After he died, his relatives (more from ignorance than malice) burned all the field notebooks, plant specimens and letters they found in his house.

I gather that Blumer's dissatisfaction with science eventually ran deep. He quit his job at the Desert Laboratory without warning, much to the inconvenience of his employer. Apparently, his colleagues there never accepted him as a peer. After he left, one of them told MacDougal, "I am certain you will eventually get more for your money than B. gave. He made too hard work of things and failed to make much of his time, in my humble opinion." And although he published twenty-one papers in botanical journals, he never achieved any status or recognition. No wonder he left science for farming.

Blumer's desire for recognition was something more than mere vanity. Recognition by peers is supposedly the major reward for work well done in science, especially in biology, where salaries are far from munificent. You might win a Nobel Prize (except in botany, where there are none); you might have a process or a species named after you; you might be elected to the National Academy of Sciences; you might be frequently cited in journal articles. But, since science mirrors our culture in piling recognition and rewards on a few superstars and ignoring everyone else, most scientists never reap any of these rewards. Yet they keep working.

If recognition truly were their main motivation, they would give up when they finally realized that none would be forthcoming. Even a donkey will stop chasing that carrot if he never gets a bite of it, I suppose. Blumer left, but others, equally obscure and apt to be forgotten, stay. I stay. I left once, and I remember well the dullness of a job that had nothing of me in it, remember even better the pain of having no home, remember best of all the joy of returning at last. Science is a big place. There's room here for technicians who pour reagents from bottles into flasks, for Nobelists who decode the secrets of our genes, for plodders who think of science as just another job, for researchers who find that science is life itself at times. Some work for money, others for recognition, but most, I suspect, work because they love it.

Something clicks whenever they draw a chemical formula or key out a plant. Something inside shouts, "Yes, this is it. This is where I'm supposed to be."

Science demands that we supply a product—our published research—and promises to reward us for it, yet it is the process, not the product, that brings the most satisfaction. We value running the bases more than wearing that World Series ring on our finger, writing the book more than stepping up to the dais for that Pulitzer Prize. The moment of the goal is evanescent. What lasts is the work of getting there.

Tongues in Trees

Find tongues in trees,

books in the running brooks,

Sermons in stone, and

good in everything.

WILLIAM SHAKESPEARE

I

A puzzling rattle drifted from the direction of the stream as Steve and I hiked down the Miller Creek trail one afternoon.

"A chain saw?" I wondered.

"Frogs," he suggested.

He was right. In the stream bed two dozen canyon tree frogs squatted around a largish pool, some on rocks in the water or on the muddy banks, others half submerged at water's edge or on floating pads of algae.

When I approached, they quieted as though I had clamped a lid on them, but in a few minutes they began chorusing again. All were evidently male, for they sang proudly, puffing out their throats into wobbling pink sacs. Surprisingly, each produced a distinctive sound: one had a high-pitched, squeaky voice, another's was deep and resonant. Most bleated like sheep, but a few quacked like ducks.

In spite of all the racket, no female frogs were enticed to join them for mating. Every so often, though, one male attempted to mate with another, pouncing upon and clasping his putative partner from behind. Tussles broke out continually around the pond as the pursued tried to convince the pursuer that mistakes had been made. They scuffled in the shallows, nipping at each other with toothless mouths until one or the other retreated. One actually succeeded in flipping another onto its back.

It all seemed vaguely familiar, somehow, but it wasn't for some time that I made the connection: their bravado and tetchiness, from the strident call for love to the virulent homophobia, reminded me of macho cowboys in a West Texas bar.

Not that frogs are strict amphibian equivalents of cowboys —but the parallel had some interesting possibilities. Certainly bleating frogs and whistling cowboys are bent on the same goal. But how far could I take it? Could I say that the frogs were insulted by the assaults of other males? Did they regard themselves as defending their honor?

A biologist would insist that my frogs (notorious for attempting to mate with any convenient object—animal, vegetable or mineral) were reacting instinctively to an inappropriate stimulus, the frog equivalent of I'm-sorry-but-you-have-the-wrong-number. But a naturalist philosopher like Joseph Wood Krutch might argue otherwise. He believed that human and nonhuman nature aren't radically different. "Is there nothing outside ourselves which is somehow glad or sad?" he asked. "Is it really a fallacy when we attribute to nature feelings analogous to our own?" Krutch didn't hesitate to imbue the lives of plants and animals with emotional meaning. Yet I wonder if this doesn't force them into a mold where they don't belong—a human mold. We could instead recognize a continuum of emotional response throughout the living world, the way we acknowledge a continuum when it comes to acuity of sight or keenness of hearing.

Krutch even attributed human emotions to landscapes. The desert for him was courageous and happy. Here, he wrote, "the contest is not so much of plant against plant as of plant against inanimate nature. The limiting factor is not the neighbor but water; and I wonder if that is, perhaps, one of the things which makes this country seem to enjoy a kind of peace one does not find elsewhere." A lovely thought—but one neatly invalidated by recent scientific findings. Plants in the desert can and do compete against one another as vigorously as plants of humid climates. The peace and happiness Krutch attributed to deserts existed in his own mind.

Another time, along another stream, we saw a garter snake

basking on a ledge. As we approached, he headed for a deep pool in the bedrock and started crawling down its vertical wall. About halfway down he lost his grip on the polished surface and tumbled into the water. He dove to the bottom, vanishing for a few moments, then resurfaced near the edge, but the wall of the pool was so steep and slippery he couldn't crawl back out. As we watched, he swam around and around, undulating like a rope, making one futile attempt after another to escape. Finally, my daughter took pity on him and hooked him out with a stick. Apparently exhausted, he lay motionless in the sun for some time. Heather asked, "Don't you think he'd be safer somewhere else?" and carried him downstream to a different pool where the sides were less precipitous and his future food supply was assured by masses of frog eggs attached to cattail stems.

The snake wasn't aware of his good fortune, I'm sure, didn't know he'd been given another chance. And fate had already issued him at least one reprieve, for we saw puncture marks on his tail as though some predator—a hawk, perhaps—had seized, then dropped, him.

There's a moral here somewhere, no doubt. But what? Look before you leap? When need is highest, help is nighest? He that is born to be hanged shall never be drowned? Nature lover Joseph Cornell has argued that we can use such incidents as paths into self-awareness. I wonder if we can. Certainly I, like the snake, have benefited more than once from a lucky reprieve. But to compare one with the other is to make a false equation. The fable of the ant and the grasshopper supposedly teaches that if you're foolish enough to sing all summer, you must go without supper all winter. But in reality ants and grasshoppers occupy different niches. The ant remains active underground all winter long and needs a cache of seeds to tide him over. The grasshopper dies at the end of the summer, so time spent storing food, even if he could, would be time wasted, hours stolen from the important business of mating and reproducing.

Nature is more than a series of Aesop's fables dramatized for our edification, and we miss the best of what she has to teach if we continually refer her incidents and scenes back to ourselves.

2

Victorian naturalists lost no opportunity to refer nature back to themselves. Everywhere they looked they found sermons in stones and books in running brooks. They believed that when we closely examine any plant or animal, we find it precisely and minutely adapted to survive and perpetuate its kind. So elaborate are these adaptations, they reasoned, it's impossible to believe they arose by mere chance; they must, therefore, have been designed by a Creator. For them the first purpose of nature study was to demonstrate the existence of God, the second, to illustrate His attributes. This kind of thinking, known as natural theology, dominated biological science in England and America until the middle of the nineteenth century. Without any trouble at all, I can find half a dozen sermons all around me. Take, for example, the Schott yucca, which late in the spring erects massive flower spikes above the sphere of swordlike leaves. The sturdy, white flowers, shaped like upside-down tulips, are pollinated exclusively by the female yucca moth. Her behavior as she does so almost surpasses belief. From the anthers of one flower she collects pollen and rolls it into a little ball that she carries under her chin. Then she flies to a flower on another plant and deposits her eggs inside the small, green ovary. Afterwards, she rubs the ball of pollen into the flower's stigma, thereby ensuring that fertile seeds will develop as food for her offspring. The yucca depends solely on the yucca moth for pollination; the moth caterpillars rely exclusively on yucca seeds for food. Neither could exist without the other.

This must surely be a prime example of God's meticulous attention to detail, a Victorian naturalist would say. What else could explain such crucial and intricate behavior in a creature so modestly equipped with intellect?

Thanks to Charles Darwin, we can explain this and all other adaptations without invoking the participation of a Creator. In *The Origin of Species*, Darwin presented massive amounts of data to support his theory that adaptations arose not by special creation but by natural selection. A population of living organisms is variable, so his argument ran, some variations being useful, others detrimental. Animals and plants burdened with detrimental variations—poor eyesight, overly conspicuous coloration, extra appendages—will quickly be caught by predators or won't be able to compete effectively for food or mates. They won't survive. Organisms with beneficial variations—camouflage coloring, great speed, unusual sex appeal—find it easier to obtain food, mates and other necessities. They *will* survive, and, more important, they will pass their adaptive characteristics to their offspring. Slowly, over millions of years, extremely intricate structures and behaviors can evolve, even behaviors as complex as the yucca moth mindlessly rubbing pollen into the stigma of a yucca flower.

In providing a new way to think about nature, Darwin's theory of natural selection proved to be the death of sermons in stones. Theologians could no longer claim that nature provided evidence of a benevolent and intelligent Creator: natural selection was, by definition, neither benevolent nor intelligent. It involved instead a struggle for survival that most organisms were bound to lose, often in what seemed a useless or cruel or painful way.

The eye-opening possibilities of evolutionary thinking are, to my mind, far more interesting than the dead-end certainties of natural theology. When we look at yucca moths and yucca as evolutionary biologists instead of Sunday-school teachers, questions tumble through our minds. Does the bell shape of the yucca flower have something to do with the way it's pollinated? Why must the flowers be so large and substantial? How many seeds must one yucca plant produce to ensure that enough will escape the devouring caterpillars? How do the caterpillars cope with the noxious chemicals that yuccas contain? Each of these questions could lead to four more queries and each of them to another four and so on, until their ramifying branches enveloped the animate and inanimate worlds. Exploring these questions, we look into the heart of nature.

Again and again, like the yucca and its moth, plants and animals have evolved in concert, an iterative process in which each reinforces advantageous developments in the other. Flowers pollinated by hummingbirds abound in Arizona—fifty species in a dozen different plant families. Despite this taxonomic diversity, their morphological diversity is not especially notable. Just the opposite, in fact. As they evolved, these fifty species converged on a pattern that hummingbirds could quickly recognize and easily exploit—a red flower with a long, narrow tube, a small mouth and a pocket of nectar at the bottom. This design enables a hummingbird to hover in front of the flower while probing it with her darning-needle bill. The red color acts as an obvious signal, and, in fact, red so appeals to hummingbirds that they compulsively investigate red objects of any shape and size, from a Swiss Army knife to a ground cloth.

The intricacy and complexity of adaptations never ceases to fascinate me. There is a fish that inveigles prey within easy reach by wiggling the lure on its forehead; a bog plant that traps flies inside its leaves, then dissolves them for the nitrogen they contain; a caterpillar that feeds on poisonous milkweeds, then turns into a poisonous butterfly that birds avoid; an innocuous butterfly that, by imitating its poisonous associate, is also avoided by birds. It's doubly startling, therefore, to read Krutch's statement that adaptation is a cold word. "Its connotations are mechanical and it alienates us from a life process which is thereby deprived of all emotional meaning. . . . Let us not say that this animal or even this plant has 'become adapted' to desert conditions. Let us say rather that they all have shown courage and ingenuity in making the best of the world as they found it."

By reserving words such as "courage" and "ingenuity" for ourselves, Krutch argues, and choosing passive terms like "adaptation" for other organisms, we separate ourselves from the great chain of life. To a biologist, however, adaptation is not forbiddingly mechanical but wonderfully diverse and fascinating. The evolution of lungs, prehensile tails, webbed feet, compound eyes, complicated toxins and venoms, are steps in the history of certain organisms just as the invention of leavened bread, domesticated wheat, fired pottery and alloyed steel are in our human history. Instead of calling plants courageous, let's turn it around. Let's regard adaptation as an active, beautiful, creative, life-affirming process, one as characteristic of people as of kangaroo rats and water lilies.

3

The natural world brims with metaphor. A scraggly pinyon clinging to a sandstone cliff, its roots sunk deep into invisible cracks in the rock, reminds us that we, too, must sink deep roots to thrive. The manzanita whose seeds must burn before they can germinate tempts us to believe that we too must pass through fire if we are to come to fruition. The slow, deliberate opening of the evening primrose cannot be forced if the flower is to bloom; just so should we remember that all things happen in their own good time.

In truth, though, nature doesn't teach us how to live. Whose example are we to follow—the owl that drops upon its prey with silent wings and tears living flesh with beak and talons? Or the wasp that lays her eggs on a paralyzed spider so her offspring can dine in sumptuous comfort?

I once saw literally thousands of red and yellow beetles scurrying over the coarse sand of a desert wash. Many were mated, the tips of their abdomens welded together. One in every pair scrambled backward as they wandered here and there, always in tandem. Other pairs fought, struggling with flailing legs and antennae to no purpose that I could see or understand. Still others clambered onto wildflowers and gnawed on the tender leaves and petals. It was a beetle world, and I felt distinctly out of place. Yet when I returned two days later, all the beetles were gone. It seemed like an immense practical joke so complicated that the laugh at the end could hardly have been worth the trouble. These beetles ate, copulated, mixed with others of their kind, avoided their enemies—yet at most this frenetic activity lasted only two days. This was life reduced to its most basic: eating and mating and producing young.

Biologically speaking, there need be no more to life than this. If we ask, "Why are we here?" biology can only answer, "Because we evolved." If we inquire, "What is our purpose?" biology tells us "To reproduce." But answers that satisfy when applied to the so-called lower organisms appall when fitted to human beings.

Science cheerfully admits itself helpless in these matters. The describable, the visible, the calculable: that's what scientists are comfortable with. Soul, mind, life—these concepts the scientist cannot define, therefore can't explain. Evolutionary ecologist Ernst Mayr says that "The words 'life' and 'mind' . . . refer merely to reifications of activities and have no separate existence as entities. 'Mind' refers not to an object but to mental activity. . . . Life, likewise, is simply the reification of the processes of living. . . . There is no such thing as an independent 'life' in a living organism."

Paradoxically, as humans we experience ourselves as possessing souls and minds, as containing a life that somehow departs when we die. But biologically speaking, these are metaphors, not facts.

The answer to why we exist cannot be found in a test tube, nor will mathematical formulas tell us how to live our lives. Even the metaphors and parables we find in the natural world are not much help, since they are projections of what we already know or believe. Some thinkers exalt philosophy over science as a way of finding answers to the ultimate questions, as do all religions, but this, I think, sets up a false dichotomy. The choice is not one or the other; it's both together. And not just philosophy and science but religion and art, too, and whatever else we poor humans can invent to make sense of our few days on this planet.

Does nature mean? The scientist says no, the poet says yes, and the writer of natural history, balancing between the two on a rope of words, hopes to bridge the gap.

The Dancer and the Dance

O body swayed to music, o brightening glance,
How can we know the dancer from the dance?

WILLIAM BUTLER YEATS

An artisan learns to love her tools: the potter cherishes the wooden crescent used to smooth the curved clay surface, the painter has her favorite brushes, the carpenter delights in the heft of his adz. So it is in any discipline. We learn to love the tools that serve us well, in part because we give the best of ourselves to them. In this way I love the five tattered field notebooks I accumulated while working in the Rincon Mountains. They started out as pristine blank books with clean cloth covers and tightly sewn signatures, but, since I habitually marked my place with my pen and frequently pressed delicate plants between the back pages, they soon became hunchbacked and gritty. I value them no less for that.

I regard them as my own, but really they don't belong to me; they belong to the ages, as does every piece of scientific writing. Laboratory notes, data sheets, diaries, case histories, notes from reading and brainstorms scribbled on the stray scrap of paper— all such private writings should end up as part of the public record, as did Charles Darwin's famous "species notebooks," his correspondence with colleagues, even his deeply personal letters to his wife. Just as Beethoven's musical notebooks show how he developed his musical ideas, Darwin's private papers give us insights into his scientific growth. Even quite obscure biologists might find succeeding generations eager to peruse their field notebooks. The only way to prevent posthumous prying is to destroy your papers, a questionable act that smacks of fear of exposure. Better to resign yourself to the fact that privacy is not valued in science, is not even a consideration, and cut your coat accordingly.

I don't obey my own good advice, for my field notebooks inextricably tangle the personal and the public. Many scientists seal off their notebooks from their personalities, less for privacy than to foster an illusion of objectivity. Their notebooks are businesslike accounts of the work at hand, just the facts and nothing more. Over the years, my field notes have evolved beyond the basic facts, and I might write a paragraph of description, or note the birds I saw, or develop an hypothesis around my observations. Sometimes I even use my notebooks as a diary, and, unorthodox as this is, it seems the best way to avoid the schizophrenic split that scientists often impose upon themselves, a schism between the work and the person as if it were possible to separate the two.

The dancer is the dance, and the poet is the poem, some biographers imply. But is the science the scientist? Does the practice of science enable us to tap a deeper wisdom the way writing a poem might, and if so, can we really call it science?

Artists work without apology from their personal experience. Anne Truitt, the sculptor, wrote, "Artists have no choice but to express their lives. They have only, and that not always, a choice of process. This process does not change the essential content of their work in art, which can *only* be their life."

It's not so widely recognized that scientists, too, work from personal experience. My wildflower childhood somehow stamped me for good, made it inevitable that I would return to botany sooner or later. This is true of every biologist I know. While other children watched television, we were up in the woods or down on the beach or out in the vacant lot, turning over boards and rocks, picking flowers, stalking grasshoppers.

Nobel Laureate Sir Peter Medawar said that there's no such person as the obligate scientist. "Most people who are in fact scientists," he insists, "could easily have been something else instead." This cool and dispassionate statement is just what a scientist *would* say, and it could well be true of engineers, physicists, astronomers and chemists, whose lives may be as formulaic as their work (although I doubt it), but for biologists it is utterly false. Childhood decides it for us. Now, as working scientists, we follow the dictates of our minds, but in becoming biologists, we obeyed the impulses of our hearts.

Personal experience also ineluctably influences the observations scientists make, the hypotheses they form and the conclusions they reach. Alexander Skutch, for example, a botanist turned ornithologist, believes that predation is the greatest source of evil in the natural world. He does not accept that the food chain is a chain of life as well as death, that in order to survive, the dragonfly eats the gnat, the frog eats the dragonfly, the snake eats the frog, the skunk eats the snake, and the owl eats the skunk. Where most biologists would argue that predation is necessary, because without it some animal populations would multiply until they died of starvation while others would devour and eventually destroy their habitat, Skutch believes that evolution might well have taken a different course so that more organisms would live in harmony and fewer would prey upon one another. I suspect that his conclusions grew out of his personal experience— especially finding long-watched nests and nestlings destroyed by snakes and other predators.

One reason I am a botanist instead of a mammalogist or an entomologist is that, like Skutch, I find it difficult at times to accept nature as it is. Investigating a flapping noise in a patch of weeds, I was sickened to see a praying mantis devouring a butterfly headfirst as the butterfly's wings beat the air. I can't remain detached at such times. I felt anguished for the butterfly, although it would have been as logical to rejoice for the mantis.

I cannot even be objective about plants. A kind of botanical snobbery, combined with the simply human tendency to gravitate toward the unique as opposed to the ordinary, makes me love rare plants more than common ones. I might have admired the common creosote bush for its toughness, its ability to survive heat, drought and frost, its shiny, resinous leaves, its stiff yellow flowers, but instead I despised it for years because there was almost no place in the desert where it didn't grow. Then I went to West Africa and saw mile after mile of manmade desert, land where every grain of topsoil had been blown or washed away, every tree lopped for firewood and every blade of grass devoured by goats or cattle. When I returned to our creosote-bush–covered desert where miles of land serve no purpose but to exist, then I found beauty even in the ubiquitous creosote bush. Objectivity? I think not.

It is human nature to take sides. But what becomes of the much vaunted objectivity of science and scientists if certain plants, insects or animals can make us shudder? Our objectivity is a chimera. The human mind is not objective: emotions suffuse every thought we have. Frequently, I am aware that my point of view may be based not on facts and logic but on desire and optimism, or anger and envy. At times I find myself enthusiastically espousing a particular hypothesis, not because it best fits the facts at hand, but because it is appealing or intricate or fashionable or, worst of all, because *I* thought of it. Too often scientists believe they have achieved objectivity when all they've done is to suppress any recognition of subjective impulses and desires, or, as my husband says, clothed their biases in the proper jargon. A scientist who claims to be perfectly objective about his research is either fooling himself or has so little passion for his studies that he might as well be working on an assembly line.

Sometimes a scientist's biases are harmless—temporarily misleading and easily corrected by later researchers. Forrest Shreve, the desert's greatest plant ecologist, completely overlooked the effect of rodents on paloverde seedlings, most likely because mammals did not interest him. Decades later, a young, upcoming ecologist named Joe McAuliffe discovered what Shreve missed: rodents devour large numbers of the tender seedlings and have a significant impact on paloverde mortality. Joe, by virtue of his background in zoology, was peculiarly suited to such a discovery.

Other biases are more pernicious. Highly respected during

his lifetime, the British psychologist Sir Cyril Burt accumulated massive amounts of data to "prove" that heredity is far more important in determining intelligence than environment. After he died, an alert investigator showed that much of Burt's research was fraudulent: sometimes he had manipulated his data, other times he had invented it. But the damage was already done; Burt's work had already been used to foster racism; obviously, if intelligence was largely inherited, blacks and other minorities who performed poorly on standard intelligence tests were beyond help or hope, and no resources should be wasted in educating them.

Bias permeates to the heart of the scientific method. In designing and carrying out experiments, scientists see themselves as objectively gathering data. If questioned, most would insist that data simply emerge as nature is unveiled through the scientific approach, like a photograph appearing in the developing bath. But raw data do not exist out there somewhere waiting to be discovered and described. The scientist evokes them within the framework of an experiment, and this very framework is the product of his or her mind.

Even as it investigates external, objective phenomena, the mind cannot escape itself. Maybe the scientist differs less from the artist than we thought.

Scientists, of course, are as subject to the same tugs of ambition, the same animosities and rivalries, the same hungers for recognition as the most temperamental artist. This is not news to anyone except, perhaps, scientists themselves. Nevertheless, temperament is still frowned upon in scientific circles; its cultivation is not encouraged; its display is subtly punished. Unlike artists, who are expected to lead flamboyant lives—Edna St. Vincent Millay and her lovers, Vincent Van Gogh and his madness, Ernest Hemingway and his brawls—scientists are seen as drearily conventional, as stodgy and unimaginative as roast beef and mashed potatoes. Medawar has actually said that no good can come of a scientist's leading a Bohemian life. I think of Charles and Emma Darwin dutifully churning out their large Victorian family, or of Barbara McClintock, a Nobel Prize winner, living monastically as she worked on the genetics of corn.

Not all scientists lead dull, predictable lives. Two I know are notorious womanizers, and a third seems to see himself as a guru of some sort. I wouldn't, however, argue that the irregularity of their lives contributes to their science, and this, as Medawar pointed out, is the crux of the matter. Anything that happens to an artist, from picking up a frosty newspaper in the driveway when Venus is low in the morning sky, to recovering from desertion by his own true love, is material for art. The scientist, who is just as likely to pick up a frosty newspaper or be left by a lover, can do nothing with the experience but rejoice or suffer, as the case may be. The poet, upon learning of a bird that earns its living by dropping bones upon rocks so as to crack them open and expose the marrow, will seize the idea, maybe even find a metaphor for her own condition. The biologist, learning of the same bird, wonders how many other species have discovered that same niche, how much competition for bones the bird encounters, whether the bird has a bill especially adapted for extracting marrow. Artists create from an internal world, and even when an artist gazes upon nature, the questions she asks and answers in her art refer to internal states. If a poet sees an osprey swoop into the crest of a wave and arise with a gleaming fish in its talons, an emotion is evoked to be explicated in a poem or song. The osprey and fish are, in T. S. Eliot's terms, the objective correlative: they are external objects that correspond to internal states. For the scientist, the fish hawk and its catch correlate to nothing but themselves. It does a biologist no good to ask, upon seeing an osprey catch a fish, "How does this make me feel?" Not that she feels nothing: her response may be even more exalted than the poet's, knowing as she does that millions of years of evolution have fitted the osprey so precisely to its task that it could survive no other way.

Here we come to the heart of science and the scientific attitude. Feelings are not science. Let's suppose that our hypothetical biologist, deeply concerned about the long-term effects of

DDT and other pesticides on ospreys, has come to this stretch of sandy coast to investigate their nesting success. As she works, she must keep her gaze turned steadfastly outward upon the nesting ospreys and the speckled eggs wedged among the twigs; she must report what she finds as honestly as possible, trying (often unsuccessfully) to be conscious of her own biases.

Even so, beneath this scientific attitude is another level—the feelings that have brought her here. Everything in her life has led to this moment: childhood birding excursions with her father; rescuing a baby dove from the cat and raising it on oatmeal and peanut butter; forty units of ornithology and biology at the university; the knowledge that developers want to bulldoze this strip of coastal desert for a luxury hotel. She can leave none of this behind. It is as much a part of her as her hair or her wrists. Even in science, we cannot distinguish between the dancer and the dance; they spin together forever, as inseparable as paint and painting, words and poem.

Notes

Text page numbers are indicated in boldface.

COMING HOME

4 Annual rainfall in the Rincon Mountains varies from about 13 inches at the bottom to 28 inches at the top.

7 Willis Linn Jepson's *A Manual of the Flowering Plants of California* (Berkeley: University of California Press), originally published in 1925, has been superseded by Philip Munz and David Keck's *A California Flora with Supplement* (Berkeley: University of California Press, 1968. That excellent and endearing little book, *How to Identify Plants*, was written by H. D. Harrington and illustrated by L. W. Durrell (Chicago: Swallow Press, 1957).

COLLECTIONS

13 John Xántus's collections are detailed in Ann Zwinger's *John Xántus: The Fort Tejon Letters, 1857–1859* (Tucson: University of Arizona Press) 1986. Thoreau mentions these pieces of limestone in *Walden*. In *The Book of Concord: Thoreau's Life as a Writer* (New York: Viking, 1982), William Howarth describes Thoreau's collections.

14 The Edna St. Vincent Millay quote comes from *God's World*.

15–17 The classic biography of Edward Palmer is Rogers McVaugh's *Edward Palmer, Plant Explorer of the American West* (Norman: University of Oklahoma Press, 1956). Joseph and Nesta Dunn Ewan, in *Biographical Dictionary of Rocky Mountain Naturalists* (Boston: Dr. W. Junk, 1981), sketch the lives of Friedrich Adolph Wislizenus, Asa Gray and Edward L. Greene. Samuel B. Parish (1908),

"Fremont in Southern California," (*Muhlenbergia* 4:57–62), is one of many who have described the exploits of this explorer and politician. David Douglas, primarily a plant explorer of the Pacific Northwest, met his macabre end in Hawaii. John and Sara Lemmon's collecting work is detailed in Frank S. Crosswhite's (1979) " 'J. G. Lemmon & Wife,' Plant Explorers in Arizona, California and Nevada" (*Desert Plants* 1:12–21). In *Some American Medical Botanists Commemorated in Our Botanical Nomenclature* (Troy, New York: Southworth, 1914), Howard A. Kelly summarizes the life of George Engelmann. Frank S. Crosswhite and Carol D. Crosswhite (1985) have written about fierce Kate in "The Plant Collecting Brandegees, with Emphasis on Katharine Brandegee as a Liberated Woman Scientist of Early California" (*Desert Plants* 7:128–139, 158–162). One account of Alice Eastwood's life is Carol G. Wilson's *Alice Eastwood's Wonderland* (San Francisco: California Academy of Science, 1955). Readable biographies of several of these and other plant collectors can also be found in Joseph Ewan's *Rocky Mountain Naturalists* (Denver, Colorado: Denver University Press, 1950).

ROSES BY OTHER NAMES

20 Arizona botanists rely on the keys contained in Thomas H. Kearney and Robert H. Peeble's *Arizona Flora* (Berkeley: University of California Press, 1960).

21 One Latin name per plant is the ideal. In practice, certain species, classified again and again, end up with a string of Latin names trailing behind them like a comet's tail. The principle remains the same, though: only one of these names is valid; the rest are, as taxonomists say, reduced to synonymy.

22–23 This account of Linnaeus's life and work relies heavily on two sources: Wilfred Blunt's *The Compleat Naturalist: A Life of Linnaeus* (New York: Viking, 1971), and, within that book, the appendix by William T. Stearn, titled "Linnaean Classification, Nomenclature, and Method." Stearn also recounts the Reverend Samuel Goodenough's criticism of the Linnaean system. Mary Moorman reports on Dorothy Wordsworth's botanical efforts in *Journals of Dorothy Wordsworth* (Oxford: Oxford University Press, 1971).

24 E. Hunn in "The Utilitarian Factor in Folk Biological Classifi-

cation" (*American Anthropologist* 84 [1982]: 830–847) points out that it
is not just "good" plants and animals that receive folk names; harmful organisms may also be named. The information on Indian-root
comes from E. S. Hunn and D. H. French, "*Lomatium*: A Key Resource for Columbia Plateau Native Subsistence" (*Northwest Science*
55 [1981]: 87–94).

25–26 Peter H. Raven, Brent Berlin and Dennis E. Breedlove
argue in "The Origins of Taxonomy" (*Science* 174 [1971]: 1210–1213),
that completing a world survey of organisms is "patently impossible" and of doubtful utility. Their paper has provided much of
the inspiration and information for this brief discussion of folk and
biological taxonomy. Joseph Wood Krutch's reproof of taxonomists
comes from *The Desert Year* (New York: W. Sloan, 1952). *The Man
Who Mistook His Wife for a Hat and Other Clinical Tales* contains Oliver
Sacks's fascinating account of a case of visual agnosia (New York:
Harper and Row, 1985).

BACKWARDS INTO SPRING

31 These germination data for winter annuals come from two
sources: Janice Beatley's "Phenological Events and their Environmental Triggers in Mojave Desert Ecosystems" (*Ecology* 55 [1974]:
856–863); and "Ecology of Desert Plants. IV. Combined Field and
Laboratory Work on Germination of Annuals in the Joshua Tree
National Monument," a 1956 paper by M. Juhren, F. W. Went and
E. Phillips (*Ecology* 37:318–330).

PULLING SUMMER FROM THE GROUND

35 The Emily Dickinson quote comes from "A Narrow Fellow in
the Grass."

40–41 Olof Arrhenius published his model for species diversity
in "Species and Area" (*Journal of Ecology* 9 [1921]: 95–99). Organ
Pipe Cactus National Monument supports 522 species in 522 square
miles, the Rincon Mountains, 986 species in 200 square miles. For
further details, see my "Flora of Organ Pipe Cactus National Monument" (*Journal of the Arizona-Nevada Academy of Science* 15 [1980]:
1–11, 33–47); and "Flora and Vegetation of the Rincon Mountains,
Pima County" (*Desert Plants* 8 [1987]: 51–94), written with Steven P.

McLaughlin. A more technical analysis of species diversity among Arizona floras can be found in our 1982 paper, "Plant Species Diversity in Arizona" (*Madroño* 32:225–233).

41–42   The Krutch quote comes from *The Desert Year*. The Thoreau quotes come from *The Heart of Thoreau's Journals*, Odell Shepard, ed. (New York: Dover, 1961).

THE ISLAND LIFE

44   Mica Mountain reaches 8,666 feet, Rincon Peak, 8,482 feet.

47   C. P. Pase and R. Roy Johnson compiled a flora for the Sierra Ancha, Gila County, Arizona: *Flora and Vegetation of the Sierra Ancha Experimental Forest*, USDA Forest Service Research Paper RM-41 (1968).

48–50   Forrest Shreve speculated about ancient vegetation change in the *Carnegie Yearbook* for 1917 (Washington, D.C.: Carnegie Institution of Washington) and in "A Comparison of the Vegetational Features of Two Desert Mountain Ranges" (*Plant World* 22 [1919]: 291–307). The best source for information on packrat middens and the stories they tell is *Packrat Middens: The Last 40,000 Years of Biotic Change*, edited by Julio L. Betancourt, Thomas R. Van Devender and Paul S. Martin (Tucson: University of Arizona Press, 1990).

51   The other moisture-loving species that I failed to find were *Alnus incana* subsp. *tenuifolia*, *Habenaria limosa*, *Agrimonia striata* and *Humulus americanus*. I considered two other hypotheses as well: that certain species had been eliminated when the pond at Manning Camp was bulldozed and dammed; and that I had simply overlooked wild rose and the other five. In the end, I decided that the pattern best fits the hypothesis that these six species died following climatic change.

52   The Shreve quote comes from his classic study of the Santa Catalina Mountains, *The Vegetation of a Desert Mountain Range as Conditioned by Climatic Factors*, Carnegie Institution of Washington Publication no. 217 (1915).

SCIENCE WITH A CAPITAL S

54   I am deeply indebted to Ernst Mayr's discussion of experimental and observational science in *The Growth of Biological Thought: Diver-*

sity, Evolution, and Inheritance (Cambridge, Massachusetts: Belknap, 1982). The Mayr quote is from this same source.

55–56 The history of the permanent plots on Tumamoc Hill is summarized by Deborah E. Goldberg and Raymond M. Turner in "Vegetation Change and Plant Demography in Permanent Plots in the Sonoran Desert" (*Ecology* 67 [1986]: 695–712).

57–58 My intent here is not to denigrate birders, many of whom, through the Audubon Society and other conservation organizations, contribute countless hours and dollars to the preservation of wildlife and wildlands. My point is simply that the birder's life-list is not a scientific undertaking.

58 W. H. Camp, "Distribution Patterns in Modern Plants and the Problems of Ancient Dispersals" (*Ecological Monographs* 17 [1947]: 160–183), presented many maps of plant distribution showing how plant families and genera had been stranded on different continents after Gondwanaland, the massive shield comprising South America, Africa, Madagascar, India and Australia, broke apart. At least sixty-four genera occur in both South America and Africa, and at least twenty-eight are split between South America and New Zealand-Australia. Camp correctly posited that "such a sequence of events will demand a former somewhat different . . . alignment of the land masses of the Southern Hemisphere than now exists."

THE CACTUS AND OTHER ANOMALIES

67 The Rincon Mountains lie within the Sonoran Desert, a vast arid tract in southern Arizona, southeastern California and the adjacent Mexican states of Sonora and Baja California. This is, perhaps, one of the most studied of the world's deserts. Readers seeking further information are encouraged to peruse Forrest Shreve's *Vegetation of the Sonoran Desert*, Carnegie Institution of Washington Publication no. 591 (1951). Popular accounts can be found in many sources. Among the recent ones are Ann Haymond Zwinger's *The Mysterious Lands* (New York: Truman Talley/E. P. Dutton, 1989); John Alcock's *Sonoran Desert Spring* (Chicago: University of Chicago Press, 1985), as well as his *Sonoran Desert Summer* (Tucson: University of Arizona Press, 1990); and two books by Gary Paul Nabhan: *Gathering the Desert* (Tucson: University of Arizona Press, 1985), and *Saguaro:*

A View of Saguaro National Monument and the Tucson Basin (Tucson: Southwest Parks and Monuments Association, 1986).

68   The argument that the vegetation around Tucson is not truly a desert plant community goes back to 1913 and has been revived by Raymond M. Turner and David E. Brown, "Sonoran Desert-scrub" (*Desert Plants* 4 [1982]: 181–221). To make my point, I fear, taken liberties. Ray Turner and Dave Brown have both spent innumerable hours hiking in the desert in midsummer.

68   Daniel T. MacDougal reported on barrel cactus in the 1915 volume of the *Carnegie Yearbook* (Washington, D.C.: Carnegie Institution of Washington).

71   The argument that columnar cacti (including saguaros) branch to increase photosynthetic surface area comes from Martin L. Cody, "Structural Niches in Plant Communities," pp. 381–405 in J. Diamond and T. J. Case, eds., *Community Ecology* (New York: Harper and Row, 1986). Park S. Nobel, "Influences of Photosynthetically Active Radiation on Cladode Orientation, Stem Tilting, and Height of Cacti" (*Ecology* 62 [1981]: 982–990), made a similar argument for prickly pears. Another reason saguaros branch may be to increase the number of flowers and fruits, hence the number of seeds produced per plant, according to Warren F. Steenbergh and Charles Lowe, *Ecology of the Saguaro: II. Reproduction, Germination, Establishment, Growth, and Survival of the Young Plant*, National Park Service Scientific Monograph Series No. 8, Government Printing Office, Washington, D.C. (1977).

72   The Forrest Shreve quote comes from his *The Cactus and Its Home* (Baltimore: Williams and Wilkins, 1931). He was probably the first ecologist to argue that cactus spines evolved for physiological reasons. Park Nobel reported his research on spines in *The Cactus Primer*, written with Arthur C. Gibson (Cambridge, Massachusetts: Harvard University Press, 1986). The adaptiveness of spines on plants is a matter of controversy among ecologists. S. M. Cooper and N. Owen-Smith, "Effects of Plant Spinescence on Large Mammalian Herbivores" (*Oecologia* 68 [1986]: 446–455), found that plant thorns and spines cause browsing ungulates (domestic goats, kudu and impala) to take smaller bites, to bite more slowly and to focus more on plants with larger leaves or fewer thorns. On the other hand, D. A. Potter and T. W. Kimmerer, in "Do Holly Leaf Spines Really Deter Herbivory?" (*Oecologia* 75 [1988]: 216–221), conclude that fall webworms are deterred more by the thick leaf cuticle and tough leaf margin than they are by the spines. Whether or not spines are adaptive seems to depend on which plants and animals are being considered and on how much protection spines must confer before they are considered a defense against predators.

73 For this material on succulence and thornforest, I am indebted to Tony L. Burgess and Avi Shmida, "Succulent Growth Forms in Arid Environments," pp. 383–395 *in* E. E. Whitehead et al., eds., *Arid Lands Today and Tomorrow, Proceedings of an International Research and Development Conference* (Boulder, Colorado: Westview Press; and Tucson: Office of Arid Lands Studies, University of Arizona, 1988).

THE LAND OF OAKS

76 Photographic evidence of the demise of oaks along the lower margin of the woodland appears in James Rodney Hastings and Raymond M. Turner, *The Changing Mile: An Ecological Study of Vegetation Change with Time in the Lower Mile of an Arid and Semiarid Region* (Tucson: University of Arizona Press, 1965).

77 For life-history information about the gray-breasted jay (formerly known as the Mexican jay), I have relied on two sources: J. L. Brown, "Social Organization and Behavior of the Mexican Jay" (*Condor* 65 [1963]: 126–153); and P. W. Westcott, "Relationships Among Three Species of Jays Wintering in Southeastern Arizona" (*Condor* 71 [1969]: 353–359).

78 C. P. Pase discusses life history of Emory oak in "Survival of *Quercus turbinella* and *Q. emoryi* Seedlings in an Arizona Chaparral Community" (*Southwestern Naturalist* 14 [1969]: 149–155).

DEMOLITION DERBY

79–81 Saguaro life history and its decline in the Rincon Mountain unit of Saguaro National Monument are described in *Ecology of the Saguaro: II.* Raymond M. Turner's as-yet-unpublished studies demonstrate the recent resurgence of saguaro at the monument. Gary Nabhan, *The Desert Smells Like Rain: A Naturalist in Papago Indian Country* (San Francisco: North Point Press, 1982), describes the Papago attitude toward saguaros.

82 It had long been believed that climatic change eliminated woodlands in the vicinity of Chaco Canyon, New Mexico. Julio Betancourt, however, has shown that, more likely, the Anasazi Indians denuded the slopes of trees in their search for fuel and construction beams. See J. L. Betancourt and T. R. Van Devender, "Holocene Vegetation in Chaco Canyon, New Mexico" (*Science* 214 [1981]: 656–58) 1981; and J. L. Betancourt, J. S. Dean and H. M. Hull, "Prehistoric long-distance transport of construction beams, Chaco Canyon, New Mexico" (*American Antiquity* 51 [1986]: 370–375).

83 The Hohokam agave, *Agave murpheyi*, was cultivated on a large scale by prehistoric Hohokam and Salado Indians. Now known only from scattered populations, it is endangered by urban sprawl, according to Gary Nabhan in an article appearing in the newsletter of the Arizona Native Plant Society, "Threatened Hohokam Agaves Need Your Help" (*The Plant Press* 13 [1989]: 7).

THOMAS GRAY WAS WRONG

86–87 The classic text on pollination ecology is K. Faegri and L. van der Pijl's *The Principles of Pollination Ecology* (Oxford: Oxford University Press, 1979). Another excellent account, written for a wider audience, is *The Sex Life of Flowers*, by Bastiaan Meeuse and Sean Morris (New York: Facts on File, 1984).

87–88 Verne Grant describes hawkmoth pollination of sacred datura in "Behavior of Hawkmoths on Flowers of *Datura mete-loides*" (*Botanical Gazette* 144 [1983]: 280–84). The Emily Dickinson reference is to her poem, "I Taste a Liquor Never Brewed."

89 The Thoreau quote comes from the Odell Shepard edition of his journals.

THE BLESSINGS OF WILDERNESS

93 Thoreau said in *Walden* that in the wilderness he grew like corn in the night.

99 The Walt Whitman quote comes from Justin Kaplan's biography, *Walt Whitman: A Life* (New York: Simon & Schuster, 1980).

SEEING TRULY

101   The Annie Dillard quote comes from *Pilgrim at Tinker Creek* (New York: Harper's Magazine Press, 1974).

103   This is not to say that scientists never write myth. Famed plant ecologist Frederic Clements insisted, in *Plant Succession: An Analysis of the Development of Vegetation*, Carnegie Institution of Washington Publication No. 242 (1916), and elsewhere, that the plant community is a literal organism, like a tree or a human being. His mythic approach reinforces my point: in reading ourselves into nature, we increase the danger that we will write myth rather than science.

103–4   The Thoreau quote comes from the Odell Shepard edition of his journals. I have taken the description of mating gopher snakes from Edward Abbey's *Desert Solitaire: A Season in the Wilderness* (New York: McGraw-Hill, 1968). Unfortunately, I no longer remember where I read the suggestion that these snakes were sparring rather than courting. Karl von Frisch's bee research has been described by, among others, Friedrich G. Barth in *Insects and Flowers: The Biology of a Partnership* (Princeton, New Jersey: Princeton University Press, 1985). Marge Piercy made these wise observations in "Afterthoughts: A Conversation Between Ira Wood and Marge Piercy" *in* p. 324, *Parti-Colored Blocks for a Quilt* (Ann Arbor: University of Michigan Press, 1982).

105–6   For these details of Thoreau's "kalendar," I have relied on E. Wagenknecht, *Henry David Thoreau: What Manner of Man* (Amherst: University of Massachusetts Press, 1981); and R. D. Richardson, Jr., *Henry David Thoreau: A Life of the Mind* (Berkeley: University of California, 1986). The quotes from Thoreau's journal and the Odell Shepard quote are from *The Heart of Thoreau's Journals*.

THE GREAT PAPER MEMORY

108   This discussion of the publication process is based largely on J. R. and S. Cole's analysis in "The Ortega Hypothesis" (*Science* 178 [1972]: 368–75).

109   William Morton Wheeler is quoted in M. A. Evans and H. E. Evans, *William Morton Wheeler, Biologist* (Cambridge, Massachusetts: Harvard University Press, 1970).

109   Effie Spalding wrote about saguaros in "Mechanical Adjustment of the Saguaro (*Cereus giganteus*) to Varying Quantities of Stored Water" (*Bulletin of the Torrey Botanical Club* 32 [1905]: 57–68).

110–11   My biographical sketch of Blumer, "Jacob Corwin Blumer, Arizona Botanist," appeared in *Brittonia* 35 (1983): 197–203.

111–12   N. W. Storer, in *The Social System of Science* (New York: Holt, Rinehart & Winston, 1966), argues that the primary rewards for a scientist are the forms of visible recognition accorded by colleagues.

TONGUES IN TREES

114   The Krutch quotes are from *The Desert Year*. Krutch doubtless got his opinions about the contest of plant against inanimate nature from Forrest Shreve, who frequently denied the existence of competition among desert plants. One of many recent papers detailing desert plant competition is Joseph R. McAuliffe's "Sahuaro-Nurse Tree Associations in the Sonoran Desert: Competitive Effects of Sahuaros" (*Oecologia* 64 [1984]: 319–21).

115   Joseph Cornell has written about nature as a mirror in *Listening to Nature: How to Deepen Your Awareness of Nature* (Nevada City, California: Dawn Publications, 1987).

116   A recent scientific account of yucca pollination can be found in C. L. Aker and D. Udovic, "Oviposition and Pollination Behavior of the Yucca Moth, *Tegeticula maculata* (Lepidoptera, Prodoxidae), and Its Relation to the Reproductive Biology of *Yucca whipplei* (Agavaceae)" (*Oecologia* 49 [1981]: 96–101).

116–17   Charles Darwin's theory of natural selection, presented in *On The Origin of Species by Means of Natural Selection or the Preservation of Favored Races in the Struggle for Life* (London: Murray, 1859), is one of several theories that organize and explain the facts of evolution. A recent rival is N. Eldredge and S. J. Gould's theory of punctuated equilibria, presented in "Punctuated Equilibria: An Alternative to Phyletic Gradualism," p. 304–32 *in* T. J. M. Schopf, ed., *Models in Paleobiology* (San Francisco: Freeman, Cooper, 1972). Their theory argues that instead of proceeding gradually over long periods of time, evolution occurs during short-term events that are separated by longer periods of stasis. The two theories do not differ on whether or not evolution occurs—it has and does—but, rather, on the rate and location of evolutionary changes. My aim in the text is not to argue the merits of Darwinian gradualism against Gouldian punctuationism; I mean only to point out that when the Victorians understood the facts of evolution—understood that one could explain the human eye, say, as an example of evolution rather than of Divine creation—they abandoned natural theology. I have taken the point from Lynn Barber's *The Heyday of Natural History* (Garden City, New York: Doubleday, 1980), a delightful account of Victorian naturalists and Darwin's crushing effect upon them.

118 The classic study of the evolutionary interaction of flowers and hummingbirds is that of Karen A. Grant and Verne Grant, *Hummingbirds and Their Flowers* (New York: Columbia University Press, 1968).

118 The Krutch quote is from *The Desert Year.*

120 The Ernst Mayr quote comes from *The Growth of Biological Thought.*

120 Better minds than mine have grappled with these problems, but I am not certain that one person's solution has much applicability to another person. I tend to agree with Anais Nin, who wrote, "There is not one big, cosmic meaning for all, there is only the meaning we each give to our life, an individual plot, like an individual novel a book for each person" (*The Diary of Anais Nin, Volume 1, 1931–1934,* Gunther Stuhlmann, ed., (New York: Harcourt Brace Jovanovich, 1967). In any case, readers interested in a thoroughgoing analysis of what science can and cannot do are urged to read Peter Medawar's *The Limits of Science* (Oxford: Oxford University Press, 1984).

THE DANCER AND THE DANCE

122 The Anne Truitt quote comes from *Daybook* (New York: Pantheon, 1982), the Peter B. Medawar quote from *Advice to A Young Scientist* (New York: Harper & Row, 1979).

123 I base my discussion of Alexander Skutch on his book, *A Naturalist on a Tropical Farm* (Berkeley: University of California Press, 1980).

124–25 Forrest Shreve discussed paloverde seedlings in "Establishment Behavior of the Palo Verde" (*Plant World* 14 [1911]: 289–

296). Joseph R. McAuliffe amplified Shreve's studies in "Herbivore-Limited Establishment of a Sonoran Desert Tree, *Cercidium microphyllum*" (*Ecology* 67 [1986]: 276–280). In *Betrayers of the Truth: Fraud and Deceit in the Halls of Science* (New York: Simon & Schuster, 1982), William Broad and Nicholas Wade recount the story of Sir Cyril Burt and his fraudulent research.

125   S. C. Grover, in *Toward a Psychology of the Scientist* (Washington, D.C.: University Press of America, 1981), discusses the biases inherent in the scientific method.

Common Plant Names

About the Author

JANICE EMILY BOWERS, essayist, biographer and botanist, is the author of *Seasons of the Wind*, *A Sense of Place* and other books. She loves cats, quilts, butterflies and birds, and reads mostly biographies and murder mysteries. She and her husband, Steve McLaughlin, live in Tucson, Arizona. Together they are working on a flora of the Huachuca Mountains on the Mexican border.